The RYA Book of Navigation Exercises

The RYA Book of

Navigation Exercises

Alison Noice
James Stevens

ADLARD COLES NAUTICAL

London

Published 1997 by Adlard Coles Nautical
an imprint of A & C Black (Publishers) Ltd
35 Bedford Row, London WC1R 4JH

Copyright © Alison Noice and James Stevens 1997

First published 1997

ISBN 0-7136-4644-6

A CIP catalogue record for this book is available from the
British Library.

Typeset in 11/14pt Concorde by Falcon Oast Graphic Art
Printed and bound in Great Britain by Bell & Bain Ltd, Glasgow

The material in this book (ie chart extracts, tide tables, etc) is to be used only for the
purpose of completing the exercises and not for navigation. Whilst every effort has been
made to ensure that the contents are as accurate as possible, neither the authors nor
publishers can accept any responsibility for errors or omissions that may be found.

Contents

Foreword

'Navigation is yesterday's problem. Today we have instant access to highly accurate electronic position fixing information, so why should anyone need to learn about navigation?'

We have indeed, for the last few years, had the ability to fix our position at sea quickly and accurately, in all conditions of visibility, by day or night. But to conclude that this means that we no longer need navigational skills would be a very dangerous mistake. Ever since affordable electronic position fixing has been a feature of yacht navigation, the annual figures for Lifeboat launches to stranded yachts have shown a steady year-on-year increase.

Position fixing has never been more than a part of the navigator's problem. In the distant past, before we had accurate clocks, it posed enormous problems to the ocean voyager. Over the years we have solved these problems so that today the more significant navigational question is not 'Where am I?' but 'Where do we go from here?'

Now that we have such high levels of potential accuracy it is possible to navigate with much tighter safety margins, and this places ever higher demands on navigational skills. This book makes a significant contribution to those skills, at two important levels.

For the beginner who is learning navigation, the ability to test newly-acquired skills is probably the most important part of the learning process. For the more experienced navigator, opportunities to practice every aspect of his or her art will inevitably be limited, so a set of exercises is invaluable for keeping in practice.

There can be few people with better credentials to produce this book than James Stevens and Alison Noice. They have both been involved with teaching navigation, at all levels, for many years, so they know exactly which of the subject areas cause difficulty in the classroom. Even more importantly, they are both active and practical yacht navigators, and their work is not just about academic exercises, it carries the essential authority of the practical exponent of the navigator's art.

Bill Anderson
Training Manager
Royal Yachting Association

Introduction

These exercises are for all those wishing to brush up their navigation skills, but in particular for students on RYA shorebased courses. The papers are written to the RYA syllabus and use the same practice tables.

In each exercise the questions become progressively more advanced. If you can answer all of them you have most of the theory knowledge required to be a Yachtmaster or Coastal Skipper. Day Skippers should be able to answer the first part of each exercise.

A practice chart and tables are included in this book. No further charts or almanacs or pilot books are required.

Equipment

You will need a plotting instrument such as a Portland or Breton plotter, and dividers which you can purchase from a chandlery shop. Also a 2B pencil and a good eraser.

Accuracy

You should aim to navigate to an accuracy of 0.1 mile, and 1.0° for chartwork and 0.1 metre for tidal calculations.

At sea it is not always necessary to navigate to this level of accuracy, but a good yacht skipper knows that precise navigation in, say, fog or other adverse conditions, can greatly enhance the safety of the passage. Accurate navigation also allows the skipper to explore new and interesting ports and anchorages.

Finally, remember that the main reason for becoming more competent at sea is to gain more pleasure from the sport.

Alison Noice
James Stevens

Part I

NAVIGATION EXERCISES

1. Nautical Terms and Seamanship

1.1

Which letters refer to the following?

1	Liferaft	9	Lifebelt	17	Lifebelt light
2	Waterline	10	Forehatch	18	Keel
3	Jib luff	11	Stemhead	19	Forestay
4	Gooseneck	12	Pulpit	20	Guardrail
5	Reef pennant	13	Danbuoy	21	Stanchion
6	Clew	14	Reef point	22	Batten
7	Rudder	15	Winch	23	Jib sheet
8	Mainsheet	16	Propeller	24	Skeg

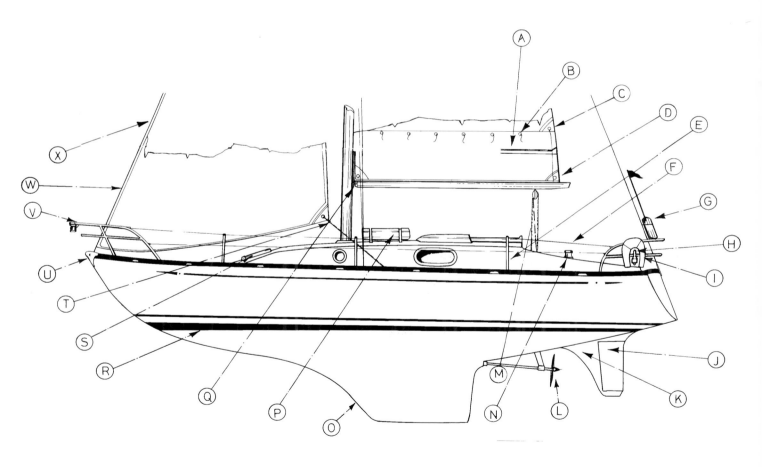

Turn to page 37 for answers

Nautical Terms and Seamanship *continued*

1.2

Which letters refer to the following?

1	Windlass	**7**	Liferaft	**13**	Stanchion
2	Stemhead	**8**	Gunwale	**14**	Bridge deck
3	Propeller	**9**	Windscreen	**15**	Rudder
4	Radar scanner	**10**	Bathing platform	**16**	Transom
5	Davit	**11**	Chine		
6	Trim tab	**12**	Guardrail		

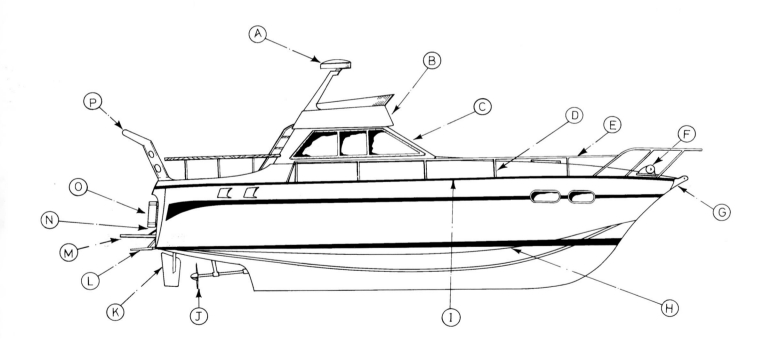

Turn to page 37 for answers

Nautical Terms and Seamanship continued

1.3

Which letters on the diagram refer to the following?

1   Chart table
2   Cockpit locker
3   Engine
4   Bulkhead
5   Heads
6   Galley
7   Companionway steps
8   Quarter berth
9   Saloon berth
10   Forepeak berth
11   Saloon table
12   Chain locker
13   Gas locker

Which numbers on the diagram refer to the following?

A   To windward
B   Astern
C   Starboard beam
D   Port quarter
E   Starboard quarter
F   Starboard bow
G   Port beam

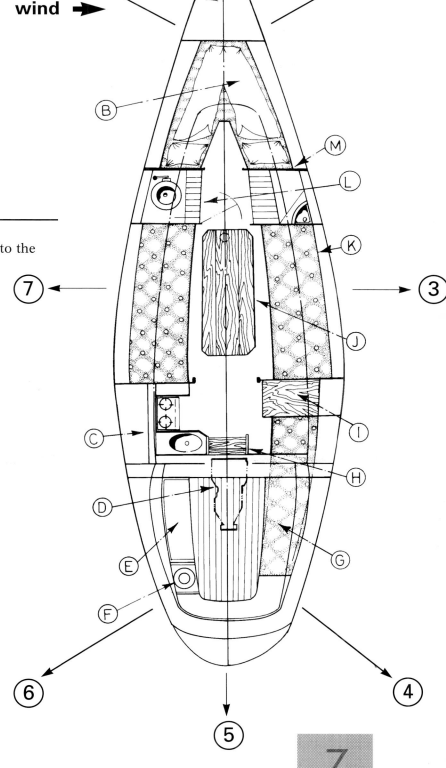

wind ➡

Turn to page 37 for answers

7

Nautical Terms and Seamanship *continued*

1.4

What are the names and uses of the following knots and hitches?

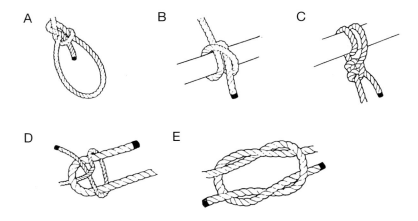

A   B   C

D   E

1.5

What are the following points of sail?

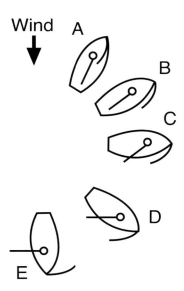

Wind   A

B

C

D

E

8

Turn to page 37 for answers

Nautical Terms and Seamanship *continued*

1.6

Draw the ropes you would use to secure the yacht against the quay. It is half tide. The range of the tide is 3 metres.

1.7

Match the controls to the effect on a power boat.

A	Starboard trim down	**1**	Bow up
B	Port trim down	**2**	Bow down
C	Outdrive aft	**3**	Correct list to port
D	Starboard trim up	**4**	Correct list to starboard
E	Port trim up		
F	Outdrive forward		

Turn to page 38 for answers

2. Chart Familiarisation

Use chart 5055

2.1

On Admiralty charts from which level

    a) are depths measured on the chart?
    b) are heights measured on the chart?

2.2

What indication is given that the Hydrographic Office publish a larger scale chart of the Dover area? What is the chart number?

2.3

On chart 5055 what is the significance of:

    a) the magenta tinted area in the Dover Straits?
    b) the green tinted area close to the shore?
    c) the purple 'tear-drop' next to some navigational buoys?
    d) the pale blue shading at sea?

2.4

What are the meanings of the following symbols?

    a) ⁜   b) ⊕   c) ◣   d) 〰   e) FS

    f) 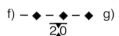   g)   h) ✳   i) ⚓   j) ⎯3kn⟶

2.5

What is the nature of the bottom in the following positions?

    a) 242°(T) Folkestone Pier light 4.2M
    b) 070°(T) Eastbourne Pier light 6M

Turn to page 39 for answers

Chart Familiarisation *continued*

2.6

What are the meanings of the symbols at the following positions?

a) 50° 42'.1N   00° 14'.9E
b) 50° 30'.0N   00° 01'.9W
c) 51° 01'.1N   01° 02'.8E

2.7

What is the **true** bearing and distance from:

a) Royal Sovereign Light Tower (50° 43'.4N   00° 26'.2E) to Beachy Head Light?
b) Cap Gris Nez Light to ZC1 Buoy (50° 44'.9N   01° 27'.2E)?
c) Bullock Bank Buoy (50° 47'.0N   01° 07'.7E) to Dungeness Light?
d) The church at Winchelsea Beach to the pub in Rye Harbour (see inset chartlet)?

2.8

The following is an extract from Notices to Mariners. Make these corrections on chart 5055.

4265* ENGLAND, South Coast - Dover Strait - Bullock Bank - Tidal Diamond

Insert tidal diamond ⟨G⟩ centred on 50° 48'.5N 01° 11'.9E on some editions of chart 5055.

Turn to page 39 for answers

3. Compass

3.1

What is the magnetic variation at 50° 30'.0°N 00° 40'.0E in 1997?

3.2

Convert these **magnetic** bearings to **true.**

   a) 093°(M) Variation 8°W
   b) 187°(M) Variation 6°E
   c) 002°(M) Variation 1°E
   d) 357°(M) Variation 3°W

3.3

Convert these **true** bearings to **magnetic.**

   a) 256°(T) Variation 4°W
   b) 009°(T) Variation 3°E
   c) 355°(T) Variation 8°W
   d) 002°(T) Variation 7°E

3.4

What is compass deviation?

3.5

A skipper notices that the deviation on a yacht's steering compass is greater when the yacht is sailing to windward in strong winds than in calm weather. What might cause this?

Turn to page 40 for answers

Compass *continued*

3.6

Complete the table below.

True	Variation	Magnetic	Deviation	Compass
231°		237°		239°
079°	3°E			076°
	4°W	151°		150°
	2°E	011°	2°W	
348°	2°W		1°E	

3.7

A helmsman heading towards Boulogne is steering to keep Boulogne North Breakwater Light in transit with the Cathedral Cupola. The steering compass reads 120°(C).

a) What is the true bearing of this transit?
b) What is the magnetic bearing with a variation of 3°W?
c) What is the deviation on this heading?

Turn to page 40 for answers

13

4. Position Fixing

Variation 3°W

4.1

Plot these GPS positions:

  a) Waypoint: Sandettie LV   068°(T)   3.2M   (bearing towards waypoint)
  b) Waypoint: 50° 30'.0N   00° 40'.0E   278°(T)   10.5M

4.2

Plot the following positions:

  a) Pointe du Touquet Light   059°(M)
     Stella Plage Church   097°(M)
     Pte du Haut Banc Light   155°(M)

  b) Varne LV   185°(M)
     S Goodwin LV   057°(M)
     Oc W R 10s light Dover breakwater   298°(M)

  c) Dungeness Light   071°(M)
     Fl R light Rye W arm   327°(M)
     Tower   006°(M)

     Which tower was used?

  d) Sandettie LV   298°(M)
     Walde Light   195°(M)
     Dunkerque Lanby   235°(M)

     How could the navigator quickly confirm
     his position in the cocked hat?

  e) Dungeness   247°(M)
     Varne LV   077°(M)

     Comment on the accuracy of this fix.

  f) Sangatte Belfry in transit with water
     tower W of Calais   144°(M)
     Depth 26m
     Tidal height 6m

4.3

A yacht is on passage up the English Channel from the SW. It is MHWS.
At 0100 the navigator raises Cap d' Alprech Light and Dungeness white light simultaneously.
The height of eye is 2m. What is the position?

4.4

A yacht skipper is on passage from Calais to Dover in moderate to poor visibility.
An electrical fault has caused a failure of all the navigation instruments including the log.
At 0200 a horn, 1 blast every 30s, is heard on a bearing of about 255°(M). A ship is seen on a SW
course. Previously all ships seen have been travelling NE. Give an approximate position.

Turn to page 41 for answers

5. International Regulations for Preventing Collisions at Sea

5.1

a) To which side do you keep in a narrow channel?
b) What do the rules state about sailing vessels and vessels under 20m in narrow channels?

5.2

a) How can you establish whether a risk of collision exists when in sight of an approaching vessel?
b) At night how can you ensure that your avoiding action is immediately obvious to the other vessel?

5.3

In the following situations a risk of collision exists. Which is the give-way vessel and what action should she take?

a)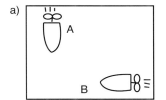

b)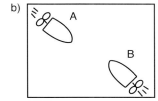

c)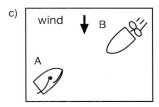

d)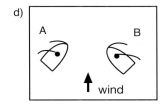

e)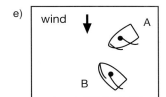

f)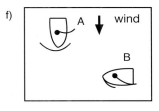

5.4

When crossing a Traffic Separation Scheme should your heading or ground track be at right angles to the traffic flow?

5.5

What sound signals are made in reduced visibility by the following craft?

a) A yacht under sail.
b) A vessel trawling.
c) A power-driven vessel underway but stopped.
d) A pilot vessel underway on duty.
e) A yacht motorsailing.
f) A 40m vessel at anchor.
g) A vessel restricted in its ability to manoeuvre.
h) A single towed vessel.

Turn to page 42 for answers

International Regulations for Preventing Collisions at Sea *continued*

5.6

What type of vessel is indicated by each of the following groups of lights? Give its probable length and aspect and whether it is underway, making way, or stopped.

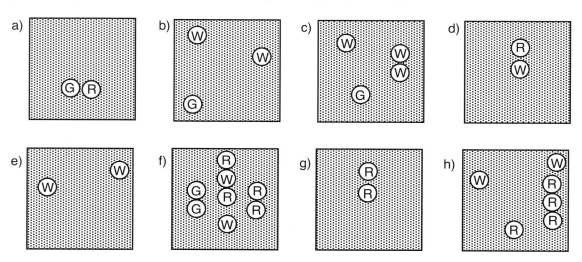

5.7

At dusk, in decreasing visibility, a yacht skipper motorsailing switches on the tricolour, steaming light and pulpit bicolour to make the yacht as visible as possible. Is this permitted in the rules?

5.8

What are the meanings of the following day shapes?

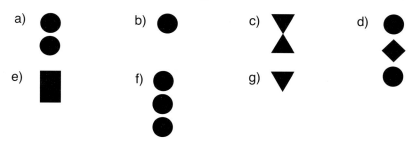

5.9

List four situations when a sailing vessel, close hauled on starboard tack, would be the give-way vessel.

Turn to page 43 for answers

6. Safety

6.1

You are skipper of the yacht *Alpha* on passage to Salcombe from the east. There are three crew on board and yourself as skipper. At 0100 hrs in heavy seas, the yacht strikes a submerged object and starts to sink. Start Point is 3 miles to the north. You decide to abandon to the liferaft. Write down the VHF message you would send.

6.2

What type of fire extinguisher would you position:

   a) Near the exits?
   b) Near the galley?
   c) In the engine space?

6.3

A rescue helicopter is overhead preparing to lift off an injured crewman. A weighted line is lowered on to the yacht. What action should the yacht crew take?

6.4

When would you direct your crew to wear:

   a) Lifejackets?
   b) Safety harnesses?
   c) What parts of the yacht are suitable for securing safety harnesses?

6.5

What type of pyrotechnic should you use when:

   a) A Search and Rescue aircraft is looking for you by day?
   b) You can see the lights of a lifeboat looking for you at night but are unsure whether the coxswain has seen you?
   c) To illuminate a man overboard at night?

6.6

List six actions to be taken as fog approaches.

Turn to page 44 for answers

7. Tidal Heights

All times are given in BST. All answers should be given in BST.

7.1

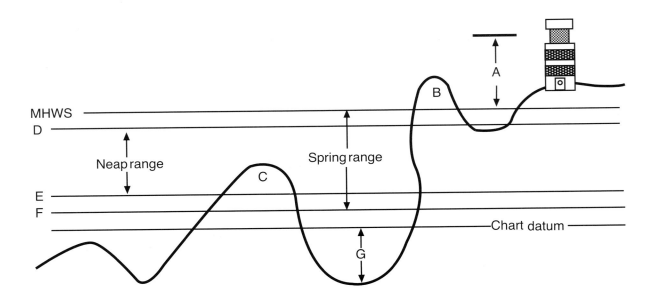

Which letters refer to the following?

1) Rock which covers and uncovers
2) Rock which does not cover
3) Charted height
4) Charted depth

5) MHWN
6) MLWS
7) MLWN

7.2

Using the tide level table on the right-hand side of chart 5055:

a) What would be the depth over the wreck of the *Ophelie* 50° 43'.7N 01° 30'.9E at MHWN?
b) What would be the depth at 50° 46'.3N 00° 01'.0E at MLWS?
c) What would be the depth of the shallowest part of the entrance channel to Rye at MHWS? (Use data from insert on chart 5055.)
d) Would the wreck at 50° 57'.5N 01° 46'.7E be visible above the surface at MLWN? Use tide levels for Calais.
e) Could a yacht with a draught of 1.2m pass over the drying area 292°(T) Pointe de Lornel LH 1.3m at MHWN with 0.3m clearance?
f) A navigator on board a 2m draught yacht, with a mast height of 16.5m, wishes to take it into Groffliers under the cable at 50° 22'.3N 01° 34'.8E. Is there any state of tide when this is possible?

Turn to page 45 for answers

Tidal Heights continued

7.3

At approximately what time does High Water Springs occur at Dover?

7.4

Give the times and heights of high and low water at Dover on the following days:

  a) Before noon on Wednesday 8 July.
  b) After noon on Friday 8 May.
  c) Before noon on Sunday 30 August.

7.5

A bilge-keeled yacht with a draught of 1.2m is moored in Dover where the charted drying height is 2.0m on the morning of Friday 3 July. At what time will she float?

7.6

At 2359 Thursday 28 May, a yacht with a draught of 1.7m is at anchor in Dover in 3.2m of water. What will be the clearance, if any, at low water?

7.7

What are the times and heights of high and low water after noon on Saturday 23 May at Dungeness?

7.8

At 0740 on Sunday 5 July a yacht grounds at the entrance to Richborough.
When will it float again? What will be the height of tide at this time?

7.9

A yacht skipper wishes to anchor off Margate at 2015 on Saturday 22 August.
If the draught of the yacht is 1.7m what is the minimum depth of water in which to anchor to ensure 1m clearance at low water?

7.10

What effect can the following have on tidal heights?

  a) High barometric pressure.
  b) Low barometric pressure and storm force winds.

Turn to pages 45–6 for answers

8. Tidal Streams

All times are given in BST. All answers should be given in BST.

8.1

Using Tidal Diamond ◁P▷ from the tidal stream table (right-hand side of chart),
what is the direction and rate of the tidal stream:

- a) 3 hours after HW Dover, springs?
- b) 1 hour before HW Dover, neaps?
- c) 2 hours before HW Dover, midway between springs and neaps?

8.2

Use the tidal stream chartlets on page 84 and 85. What will be the direction and rate of the tidal
stream:

- a) Off Beachy Head 4 hours after HW Dover at springs?
- b) South of Havengore Creek 6 hours after HW Dover at neaps?

8.3

It is Sunday 3 May and you are planning to cross the Dover Straits from Dover to Calais in your
35 ft motor cruiser which cruises at 12kn. The wind is NE4. Would it be prudent to depart before
breakfast or delay until lunchtime? Give reasons.

8.4

What is the direction and rate of the tidal stream at the following positions?
Use computation of rates table (page 87) where appropriate.

- a) South of Beachy Head at 1100 on Monday 31 August.
- b) Close to Royal Sovereign Light Tower at 0820 on Saturday 8 August.
- c) At 50° 30'.0N 00° 26'.0E at 0231 on Sunday 24 May.
- d) Approx 5½ miles WSW Cap Gris Nez at 1800 on Tuesday 9 June.
- e) Close to South Goodwin Light Vessel at 1200 on Sunday 21 June.
- f) Approx 20 miles W of Pte Du Haut Banc Light at 1800 on Sunday 9 August.
- g) Approx 3 miles off Dover at 0910 on Wednesday 6 May.

8.5

Using the tidal stream chartlets:

- a) At what time does the stream become SW-going off Dungeness during the forenoon of
Friday 24 July?
- b) At what time does the stream become N-going off Boulogne during the afternoon of
Tuesday 9 June?

Turn to pages 47 for answers

Tidal Streams *continued*

8.6

How might the tidal stream close inshore off Quend Plage (bottom right of chart) differ from the rates given for ⟨K⟩?

8.7

Would you use a tidal stream atlas or tidal diamonds in the following circumstances?

 a) Planning a passage from Calais to Rye?
 b) Shaping a course from Varne LV to Dover?
 c) Planning the departure time for a coastal passage from Folkestone to Newhaven?

Turn to pages 48 for answers

9. Estimated Position

Use chart 5055. Variation 3°W. All times are given in BST.

Use the deviation table on page 86 and the computation of rates table on page 87 for tidal stream interpolations. The chart correction in exercise 2, question 8 (Chart Familiarisation) should be entered before starting this exercise.

9.1

At 0900 a yacht skipper fixes position next to Bullock Bank buoy 50° 46'.9N 01° 07'.7E. The log reads 40.0. Plot the estimated position at 1000 when the log reads 47.0 and the course steered has been 170°(M) with no leeway. The tidal stream for this period was 036°(T) 2kn.

9.2

Using the information in the log below, plot the estimated position.

Date	Time	Log	Course	Wind	Leeway	Bar	Notes
31 August	1230	3.6	310°(M)	NE3	Nil	1010	Fix. Next to Cardinal buoy 50° 20'.4N 01° 31'.0E
	1330	10.2	310°(M)	NE3	Nil	1010	EP using ◇K◇

9.3

Using the information in the log below, plot the estimated position.

| 18 August | 1105 | 10.0 | 015°(M) | W4 | Nil | 998 | Position next to Vergoyer SW buoy 50° 26'.9N 01° 00'.0E |
| | 1305 | 19.7 | 015°(M) | W4 | Nil | 998 | EP using ◇F◇ for 1 hour then ◇H◇ |

What is the charted depth at the 1305 position?

9.4

Using the information in the log below, plot the estimated position.

| 11 July | 0300 | 20.0 | 135°(M) | S5 | 10° | 990 | Position MPC buoy 51° 06'.1N 01° 38'.4E |
| | 0400 | 26.3 | 135°(M) | S5 | 10° | 990 | EP using ◇Q◇ N Cardinal buoy ahead |

Identify the N Cardinal buoy?

Turn to pages 49–52 for answers

Estimated Position continued

9.5

Using the information in the log below, plot the estimated position.

27 June	0755	39.2	320°(M)	W4	Nil	998	Position at Ridens SE buoy 50° 43'.3N 01°19'.0E
	0955	51.8	320°(M)	W4	Nil	998	EP using ◁G▷

9.6

Using the information in the log below, plot the estimated position.

29 June	0555	10.0	135°(C)	E6	10°	1000	Decca position 51° 08'.0N 01° 31'.8E
	0715	15.9	135°(C)	E6	10°	1000	Alter course to 200°(C) to avoid ships. Leeway nil.
	0730	16.9	200°(C)	E6	Nil	1000	Alter course back to 135°(C) Decca inoperative
	0755	19.0	135°(C)	E6	10°	1000	EP using ◁P▷ for 1 hour then ◁Q▷

9.7

At 1520 Friday 22 May the yacht navigator fixes position SW of Dover at 140°(T) Shakespeare Cliff radio masts 2.2M, log 21.8. The course is 110°(C) beating against a NE wind making 10° leeway. Boat speed 5.3kn. The skipper wishes to know when to tack to avoid the Traffic Separation Scheme.

What will the log read when the yacht reaches the edge of the Traffic Separation Scheme (outer side of the magenta marking)?

Turn to pages 53–5 for answers

10. Buoyage and Lights

10.1

What is the direction of buoyage on chart 5055?

10.2

Sketch the topmarks of eight different navigational marks, the positions of which are shown in the diagram, and indicate which one should be placed in each position.

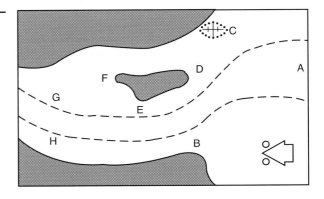

10.3

You are heading in an easterly direction when you sight a pillar buoy which is painted black at the top and yellow at the bottom. Unfortunately the topmark is missing. Do you leave the buoy on your port or starboard side?

10.4

You are sailing northwards into an estuary at night. On which side of the vessel would you leave the following lights?

  a) VQ (3) 5s   b) Fl (2) 10s   c) Oc 2 G   d) Iso 10s
  e) Q (9) 15s   f) Fl (2) R 6s   g) 2 FG (vert)

10.5

What would be the characteristic of Dungeness Light when observed from Stephenson Shoal which lies approximately 5 miles SW of Dungeness?

10.6

Beachy Head Lighthouse is shown as having a 25M light. Could it be seen from the cockpit of a small yacht at this range? Give reasons.

Turn to page 56 for answers

Buoyage and Lights *continued*

10.7

Identify the following lights which are situated on the coastline of France (use chart 5055).

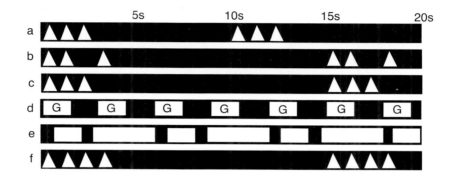

Turn to page 56 for answers

11. Course to Steer

Use chart 5055. Use Variation 3°W. All times are given in BST. All answers should be given in BST.

11.1

At 0715 a sea-angling boat is in position 50° 45'.0N 00° 32'.0E. Speed through the water 5kn. Tidal stream 260°(T) 1.2kn.

   a) What is the magnetic course to steer to the Fl Y 5s outfall buoy off St Leonards?
   b) What will be the speed over the ground?

11.2

At 0930 a motor yacht fixes position by GPS 50° 50'.0N 00° 40'.0E. Speed 15kn.
HW Dover 1300 BST. Springs. Use ⟨C⟩.

   a) What is the magnetic course to steer to CS2 buoy (50° 39'.1N 00°32'.7E)?
   b) What will be the speed over the ground?
   c) What will be the ETA?

11.3

At 1415 on Saturday 8 August a yacht is in position 50° 41'.0N 00° 15'.6E. Speed 4½kn.
Use ⟨A⟩.

   a) What is the magnetic course to steer to a position 090°(T) 1M Eastbourne Pier 2 FR lights?
   b) What will be the speed over the ground?

11.4

At 1745 on Thursday 7 May a yacht is in position 50° 38'.4N 00° 12'.0E. Speed 4½ kn.
Use ⟨A⟩ and the deviation table on page 86.
What is the compass course to steer to Newhaven W Pierhead?

11.5

At 1130 on Saturday 30 May a fishing boat is at Royal Sovereign Light Tower and intends to fish near the 19.4m wreck in position 50° 39'.7N 00° 23'.8E. Speed 8kn. What is the compass course to steer to the wreck? Use ⟨C⟩, the deviation table and the computation of rates table.

Turn to pages 57–60 for answers

26

Course to Steer *continued*

11.6

At 0907 on Thursday 16 July a yacht is at Langney Point Buoy (NE of Eastbourne Pier). Speed 5kn. Use ⟨C⟩ and the relevant tables.

a) What is the compass course to steer to the red can buoy on the S side of Royal Sovereign Shoals?

b) At what time will the yacht pass over the 5.6m charted depth on Long Shoal?

c) What would be the compass course to steer to counteract 10° leeway in a southerly wind?

11.7

At 1348 on Sunday 26 July, the following bearings are taken by a yacht's navigator:

a) Dungeness Lighthouse   038°(M)
  Eastern 18m tower   354°(M)
  Western 18m tower   329°(M)

b) What is the compass course to steer to Rye Fairway L Fl 10s buoy if leeway is estimated to be 10° in a fresh WSW wind? Speed 6kn. Use ⟨E⟩ and all relevant tables.

Turn to pages 60–1 for answers

12. Navigational Instruments

12.1

What are:

  a) The advantages of GPS over the Decca system?
  b) The disadvantages of GPS?

12.2

What is:

  a) A waypoint?
  b) Cross track error?

12.3

On a twelve hour passage across the English Channel at 5kn, is it quicker to follow the rhumb line as displayed on the GPS receiver or plot a course to steer to counter the sum of the tides and be drifted off and on the rhumb line?

12.4

A man falls overboard at night in the Dover Strait. The Man Overboard (MOB) emergency button on the GPS is activated and a course and distance is displayed back to the position where he fell in. He is not there. How would you plan your search?

12.5

You are sailing offshore when you discover that your batteries have run down to the point where you cannot start the engine. Your navigation instruments are inoperative but the yacht is still sailing well. In order to predict your landfall you need to obtain an idea of boat speed. Is there any way you can do this without instrumentation?

Turn to page 62 for answers

13. Pilotage

13.1

Approaching harbour the leading marks
are given as the circle on the rear post
and the Y on the front marker. If they appear
as shown which way would you alter course
to bring them in transit?

13.2

What is the meaning of each of the following signals:

   a) A quick flashing lamp on a building at Dover?
   b) Fixed purple light at Rye?
   c) A blue flag at Folkestone?
   d) Two blue lights at Boulogne?

13.3

You are the navigator of a motor yacht planning to enter Boulogne at night. Use the information
and chartlet for Boulogne on page 81 to write pilotage notes from outside the harbour to a
suitable berth or mooring.

13.4

You are the skipper of a yacht, draught 1.2m, on a daylight passage to Calais from the SW. It is
almost low water as you round Cap Gris Nez and the W- going stream has just begun. You decide
to stay well inshore but first have to clear the shallows and the wreck to the NE of the point.
How can you be sure you are clear of the dangers?

13.5

You are the skipper of a planing motor yacht on a cross-channel passage to Newhaven in daylight. It is 3 hours after HW Dover and the visibility has fallen to 0.5 M. To make matters worse
the GPS is inoperative and you do not have radar. Your EP is 50° 37'.6N 00° 05'.8E with a circle
of uncertainty, radius one mile. Describe your strategy for finding Newhaven.

13.6

Describe a pilotage plan at 20 knots from Sandettie Light Vessel (51° 09'.4N 01° 47'.2E) to Calais
breakwater ensuring that the Traffic Separation Scheme is crossed at the correct angle and CA2
and CA4 buoys are left to port. Assume that the tidal stream is almost slack.

Turn to pages 63–5 for answers

14. Meteorology

14.1

What are the meanings of the following terms used in weather bulletins?

a) fog   b) veering   c) falling   d) moving steadily
e) later   f) moderate   g) fair   h) imminent

14.2

Which Beaufort wind force would you expect for the following wind speeds and sea state?

a) 11 – 16 knots.   Small waves becoming larger. Frequent white crests.
b) 28 – 33 knots.   Sea heaps up, white foam, breaking waves blown into streaks.

14.3

What does Buys Ballot's Law tell you about the position of a low pressure area?

14.4

Draw a diagram to show how a sea breeze develops?

14.5

Sea fog is common in late spring and early summer in the English Channel. Why is this and what conditions will cause it to disperse?

14.6

The wind has been blowing strongly from a south-westerly direction for a number of days. What would be of particular significance to a yacht at sea if an occlusion then passed over the area with an accompanying sudden wind shift to the north west?

14.7

Use the weather map and associated forecast on page 31 to answer the following questions:

a) What would be the appearance of the sky in:
   1) Humber?   2) West Sole?

b) Why is the visibility forecasted to deteriorate in Dover? When will there be a marked improvement in visibility?

c) Why are the winds in the Thames and Humber areas expected to change by veering, whilst in the Irish Sea they are expected to change by backing?

d) If you were anchoring in area Forth, from which wind direction would you seek shelter?

e) Explain briefly the forecasts for Plymouth and for Lundy and Fastnet.

Turn to pages 66–7 for answers

Meteorology *continued*

SHIPPING FORECAST
Issued by the Meteorological Office at 1700 on Monday 25 August.

There are warnings of gales in:
Forties, Cromarty, Forth, Tyne, Dogger, German Bight, Humber, Thames, Dover, Wight, Portland, Plymouth,
Biscay, Finisterre, Sole, Lundy, Fastnet, Irish Sea, Shannon, Rockall, Malin.

General synopsis at 1300:   Vigorous low Fastnet 985 moving slowly north east with little change.

Area forecasts for the next 24 hours:

Viking, N & S Utsire	NW 4 veering E 5 or 6. Showers. Good.
Forties, Cromarty, Forth	E 3 increasing 7 to gale 8. Showers then rain. Good becoming moderate.
Tyne, Dogger	E 4 increasing 7 to severe gale 9. Rain. Good becoming poor.
Fisher, German Bight	Variable 3 becoming SE 7 to gale 8. Rain later. Good becoming poor.
Humber, Thames	SE 4 increasing 6 to gale 8 veering SW later. Rain. Moderate or poor.
Dover, Wight	SE 6 to gale 8 veering SW 7 to severe 9. Rain. Moderate or poor.
Portland	SE 6 to gale 8 veering SW 7 to severe 9. Rain. Moderate or poor becoming good.
Plymouth	SW 7 to severe gale 9 increasing storm 10 at times then veering NW. Rain. Moderate or poor becoming good.
Biscay	SW veering NW 5 or 6, but in north 6 to gale 8 occasionally severe gale 9. Occasional rain. Poor becoming good.
Finisterre, Sole	SW veering NW 7 to severe gale 9 occasionally storm 10 decreasing 5 in west later. Rain then Showers. Poor becoming good.
Lundy, Fastnet	Cyclonic 7 to severe gale 9 increasing storm 10 at times then becoming northerly. Rain. Moderate or poor.
Irish Sea	E 7 to severe gale 9 perhaps storm 10 later. Rain. Moderate or poor.
Shannon	N gale 8 to storm 10 decreasing 6 to gale 8. Rain then showers. Moderate or poor.
Rockall, Malin	NE 7 to severe gale 9 backing N 6 to gale 8. Occasional rain. Moderate or good.
Hebrides, Bailey, F Isle	E 4 or 5 occasionally 6 in Hebrides. Showers. Good.
Faeroes, SE Iceland	Variable 3 becoming NW 4 or 5. Showers. Moderate or good.

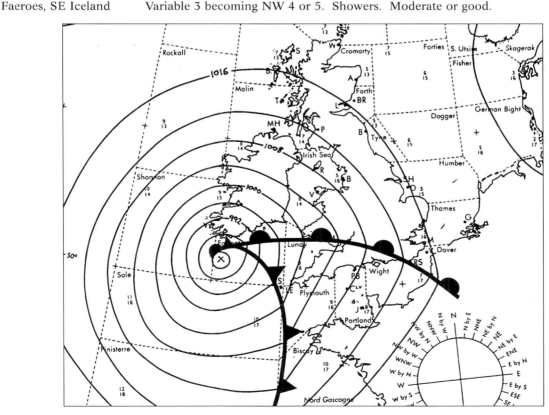

Turn to page 67 for answers

15. Passage Planning

Use extracts at the back of the book.

All times are given in BST.
For simplicity, times of tides have been rounded to the nearest ¼ hour.
Passage planning does not always result in definitive answers, sometimes there is more than one sensible option.

15.1

You are a motor yacht skipper in Newhaven Marina planning a passage to Rye on Sunday 3 May. The forecast is for light and variable winds. Cruising speed 10kn.

a) How far is the passage? What is the approximate passage time?
b) Between what times on Sunday 3 May is Rye accessible?
c) Between what times can you leave Newhaven Marina? (High water Shoreham is 1015 GMT.)
d) Between what times is the tidal stream favourable?
e) Suggest an ETD and ETA with reasons.
f) What are the hazards (i) off Beachy Head?
   (ii) between Eastbourne and Royal Sovereign?
   How could you ensure you avoid these without the use of electronic nav-aids?
g) Having arrived just to the S of Boulder Banks about 4M SW of Rye, you are unsure which of the shore features is the harbour entrance. How could you confirm the bearing of the entrance from your vessel?

15.2

You are skipper of a sailing yacht in Rye planning a passage to Groffliers 50° 22'.6N 01° 35'.8E to arrive on Sunday 30 August. Forecast NE 5. Estimated boat speed 5kn. Draught 1.5m. Mast height 10m.

a) What is the length of the passage? What is the approximate passage time?
b) Is Groffliers safe to enter in the forecast wind?
c) Groffliers must be entered at HW–1. HW Groffliers on Sunday 30 August is 0002 and 1230. Which tide is preferable?
d) When should you leave Rye?
e) You noticed earlier that there were fishing nets and buoys either side of the fairway into Rye. How can you ensure you avoid these on your departure?
f) Are there any other hazards *en route*?

Turn to page 68 for answers

Passage Planning *continued*

15.3

You are skipper of a motor sailing yacht, moored in the Bassin de L'Ouest in Calais, planning a passage to Folkestone in daylight on Thursday 11 June. Cruising speed 5kn. Your mooring in Folkestone is accessible three hours either side of HW. HW Calais is 0745 and 2030. Weather is calm.

   a) At what times can you leave the Bassin de L'Ouest in the morning?
   b) What is the length of the passage and approximate passage time?
   c) When is your mooring accessible in Folkestone?
   d) When are the tidal streams   (i) Favourable?
                                      (ii) Unfavourable?
   e) What is your ETD Calais and ETA Folkestone?
   f) What hazards are *en route*?
   g) As you approach Folkestone how can you be sure you do not enter when a ferry is about to leave?

15.4

You are skipper of a sailing yacht bound for Le Touquet. Your present position is close to Vergoyer Bank. It has been a long passage across the Channel against a SE 4–5 wind and the crew is looking forward to arriving at the restaurants of Le Touquet. An electrical fault has meant that you have not received any forecasts. The weather is fine but within the last few hours streaky cirrus clouds have appeared and the sun has become hazy. What action, if any, should you take?

15.5

You are planning a passage from Boulogne to Newhaven on Sunday 16 August. The wind is W4 forecast to veer and freshen to NW6 in the late morning. Boat speed close-hauled 5kn. Tacking angle 90°.

   a) How far is the passage   (i) Rhumb line distance?
                                 (ii) Approximate distance tacking?
   b) What is the best tacking strategy to make use of the wind veer?
   c) When should you depart?
   d) When is your approximate ETA?

15.6

You are skipper of a motor cruiser in the Bassin de L'Ouest in Calais intending to make a passage to Newhaven Marina on 14 July. You have 50 gallons of fuel. You were hoping to refuel in Calais but being a public holiday none is available.

Fuel consumption is	7kn	Displacement	2.8 mpg
	12kn	Wind against tide	2.0 mpg
	20kn	Planing	1.2 mpg

Wind NE5   HW Calais 1030 BST   HW Newhaven 2200 BST

   a) What is the distance of the passage?
   b) Will you have to refuel?
   c) What is your passage plan?

Turn to pages 68–9 for answers

16. Passage Making

Chart 5055.   Variation 3°W.   All times are given in BST.

In this exercise you are the skipper of a 32 ft yacht on passage from Etaples to Dover on Sunday 28 June. The forecast is for a fine day with W3 to 4 winds. The yacht will cruise at 5kn.

Remember that it is a requirement to cross the Traffic Separation Scheme at right angles to the traffic flow to comply with Rule 10 IRPCS.

16.1

Prepare a passage plan from Etaples to Dover considering the following:

a) Approximate distance to Dover.
b) Between which times the stream is fair to Cap Gris Nez.
c) Restrictions concerning departure times from Etaples and arrival at Dover.
d) Dangers *en route*.

16.2

The yacht leaves Etaples and steers a course of 005°(C) with no leeway. At 0800 a bearing is taken of Hardelot Plage Church 063°(M). Log reads 106.4. At 0830 another bearing is taken of the church 133°(M). Log reads 109.1. Plot the 0830 estimated position using ⟨L⟩.

16.3

At 0910 the following bearings are taken:

Boulogne North Breakwater Lt	148°(M)
Wimereux Church	086°(M)
Belfry near Ambleteuse	040°(M)

Plot the 0910 fix.

16.4

At 0930 the yacht is at Bassure de Baas Buoy (50° 48'.5N 01° 33'.2E).

a) What is the compass course to steer to ZC2 buoy (50° 53'.5N 01° 31'.0E)?
   Speed 5kn. No leeway. Use ⟨N⟩
b) What is the ETA at ZC2 buoy?

16.5

At 1100 the yacht is in position 50° 57'.6N 01° 28'.1E sailing close-hauled on port tack. Leeway estimated as 5°. Course 322°(C). Speed 5kn. If she maintains her course and speed will she pass to the E or to the W of Varne Light Vessel? Use ⟨M⟩.

Turn to pages 70–3 for answers

Part II

ANSWERS

1. Nautical Terms and Seamanship

1.1

1 P	5 C	9 I	13 G	17 H	21 E
2 R	6 D	10 S	14 B	18 O	22 A
3 X	7 J	11 U	15 N	19 W	23 T
4 Q	8 M	12 V	16 L	20 F	24 K

1.2

1 F	5 P	9 C	13 D
2 G	6 L	10 M	14 B
3 J	7 O	11 H	15 K
4 A	8 I	12 E	16 N

1.3

1 I	4 M	7 H	10 B	13 F
2 E	5 L	8 G	11 J	
3 D	6 C	9 K	12 A	

A 7	E 4
B 5	F 2
C 3	G 7
D 6	

1.4

A Bowline: For making a non slip loop in the end of a rope.

B Clove hitch: For securing the 'middle' of a rope to a spar. Both ends should be under load.

C Round turn and two half hitches: For securing a rope to a ring with minimum chafe. Can be released under load.

D Single sheet bend: For joining two ropes of unequal diameters.

E Reef knot: For reef points.

1.5

A Close hauled port tack.

B Close reach or fine reach port tack.

C Beam reach port tack.

D Broad reach port tack.

E Run goosewinged port tack.

37

Nautical Terms and Seamanship continued

1.6

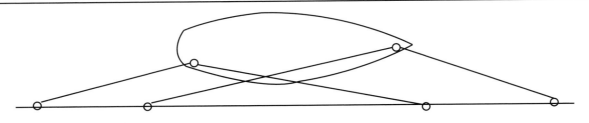

1.7

A	4	**D**	3
B	3	**E**	4
C	1	**F**	2

continued

2. Chart Familiarisation

2.1

a) Chart datum.
b) Mean High Water Springs.

2.2

A magenta box drawn around the area covered by the larger scale, chart 5061.

2.3

a) Traffic Separation Scheme.
b) Areas that are uncovered at chart datum and covered at MHWS.
c) A navigational buoy that is lit.
d) Charted depth of between 10 and 20m, enclosed by a contour line.

2.4

a) Rock awash at chart datum.
b Wreck considered to be dangerous to surface navigation.
c) Public slipway.
d) Tidal rips, overfalls.
e) Flagstaff.
f) Overhead cable with vertical clearance of 20m at MHWS.
g) Visitors' mooring.
h) Rock which covers and uncovers.
i) Windmill.
j) Ebb tide stream (with rate).

2.5

a) Sand and mud.
b) Fine sand, broken shells, small gravel and pebbles.

2.6

a) Tidal diamond ⟨A⟩.
b) Submarine cable.
c) Wreck with a charted depth of 1.6m.

2.7

a) 275°(T)   7.4M
b) 215°(T)   8.8M
c) 324°(T)   9.7M
d) 042°(T)   2.05M

2.8

Ensure that the year and the correction number are entered on the bottom left hand corner of the chart in ink.

3. Compass

3.1

3° 40'.0W in 1993 decreasing 7' annually.   3° 40'.0 – 28' = 3° 12'.0W in 1997.

3.2

  a) 085°(T)
  b) 193°(T)
  c) 003°(T)
  d) 354°(T)

3.3

  a) 260°(M)
  b) 006°(M)
  c) 003°(M)
  d) 355°(M)

3.4

Deviation is the error caused by the vessel's own magnetism. Ferrous items, particularly those which have been machined or hammered, gain a polarity which causes the ship's compass to deviate. The amount by which the compass is deviated depends on the heading of the vessel.

3.5

Probably heeling error. Measurements for deviation will have been taken with the boat on an even keel but the deviation may alter when the yacht is well heeled. Try checking your heading with the hand-bearing compass which can be deployed clear of magnetic influences.

3.6

True	Variation	Magnetic	Deviation	Compass
231°	6°W	237°	2°W	239°
079°	3°E	**076°**	0°	076°
147°	4°W	151°	1°E	150°
013°	2°E	011°	2°W	**013°**
348°	2°W	**350°**	1°E	**349°**

3.7

  a) Bearing of transit   123°(T)
       Variation   3°W
  b) Magnetic   126°(M)
       Compass reading   120°(C)
  c) Deviation   6°E   (compass reads less, so the deviation is East).

4. Position Fixing

4.1

a) 51° 08'.1N   01° 42'.5E
b) 50° 28'.5N   00° 56'.3E

4.2

a) 50° 28'.8N   01° 29'.6E.

b) 51° 05'.9N   01° 24'.2E.

c) 50° 52'.6N   00° 50'.1E
The 20m tower was used.

d) 51° 06'.0N   01° 57'.6E
The echo sounder will reveal whether the yacht is over the Out Ruytingen bank.

e) 50° 59'.4N   01° 14'.0E
The angle of cut is shallow and only two objects were used giving an inaccurate position.

f) Depth of water is 20m
50° 57'.8N   01° 43'.4E

4.3

Distance off Cap d'Alprech		19.3M
Dungeness		16.1M
Position	50° 39'.0N	01° 03'.7E

4.4

The yacht is probably entering the SW-going shipping lane in approximate position 51° 03'.0N 01° 30'.1E.

5. International Regulations for Preventing Collisions at Sea

5.1

a) Keep as near to the outer limit of the channel as possible on your starboard side.
b) Sailing vessels and vessels under 20m shall not impede the safe passage of a vessel which can safely navigate only within the channel.

5.2

a) By watching the compass bearing of the approaching vessel. If the bearing does not change there is a risk of collision.
b) By showing a different aspect of your lights to the other vessel.

5.3

a) B should sound one short blast and turn to starboard to pass astern of A.
b) A and B should both sound one short blast and both turn to starboard.
c) B should avoid A. B may turn to port to avoid passing to windward of A.
d) B on port tack should luff or gybe to avoid A.
e) A, the windward vessel, should bear away behind B or tack.
f) A, the windward vessel, should gybe and pass astern of B.

5.4

Heading.

5.5

a) One long and two short blasts at intervals not exceeding two minutes.
b) One long and two short blasts at intervals not exceeding two minutes.
c) Two long blasts at intervals not exceeding two minutes.
d) One long blast followed by four short blasts at intervals not exceeding two minutes.
e) One long blast at intervals not exceeding two minutes.
f) Bell for five seconds at not more than one minute intervals.
g) One long and two short blasts at intervals not exceeding two minutes.
h) One long and three short blasts at intervals not exceeding two minutes.

International Regulations for Preventing Collisions at Sea *continued*

5.6

a) Sailing vessel underway, under 20m in length, head on.
b) Power driven vessel underway, probably over 50m in length, starboard aspect.
c) Vessel towing, probably over 50m in length with tow under 200m, underway, starboard aspect.
d) A vessel engaged in fishing other than trawling underway, but not making way or at anchor. Any aspect, no gear extending more than 150m, any length.
e) A vessel at anchor probably over 50m in length but under 100m, starboard aspect *or* a power driven vessel probably over 50m underway, hull down or beyond visibility of side-lights, port aspect.
f) A vessel restricted in ability to manoeuvre engaged in underwater operations or dredging, stern aspect, making way, foul on its starboard side, any length.
g) Vessel not under command, underway but stopped, any aspect, any length.
h) Vessel constrained by its draught probably over 50m underway, port aspect.

5.7

No.

5.8

a) Not under command.
b) At anchor.
c) Engaged in fishing.
d) Restricted in ability to manoeuvre.
e) Constrained by draught.
f) Aground.
g) Motorsailing.

5.9

When overtaking.
When risk of collision occurs with a vessel:

- restricted in ability to manoeuvre
- not under command
- engaged in fishing
- which can only navigate safely in a narrow channel
- following a traffic lane in a traffic separation scheme

When to windward of another yacht pointing higher on starboard tack.

6. Safety

6.1

Mayday, Mayday, Mayday.
This is yacht *Alpha*, yacht *Alpha*, yacht *Alpha*.
Mayday yacht *Alpha*.
My position is 180°(T) Start Point 3 miles.
Yacht is sinking. 4 persons abandoning to the liferaft.
Require immediate assistance. Over.

6.2

  a) Dry powder.
  b) Fire blanket.
  c) Halon or other gas extinguisher.

6.3

Allow the line to earth on the yacht or in the water. Take up the slack and pull when directed. Do not attach the line to the yacht. The winchman or diver will be lowered from the helicopter. The line steadies him and guides him to the yacht. The helmsman should concentrate on the course (as previously directed by the helicopter) and not be distracted. The winchman will take charge once on deck.

6.4

  a) When there is any likelihood of abandoning the yacht or going into the water.
     At all times for non-swimmers.
     In the dinghy.
  b) Depending on the experience of the crew, in rough seas and at all times at night.
  c) Jackstays, standing rigging, mast, cleats, rings and other strong points but not guardrails or running rigging.

6.5

  a) Orange smoke or pin point red.
  b) Pin point red.
  c) White parachute.

6.6

- Fix position.
- Hoist radar reflector.
- Switch on navigation lights.
- Put on lifejacket and harness. Make sure you can release harness quickly.
  (NB The danger of falling overboard in fog is as great as not being able to unclip in a collision situation.)
- Post lookouts to listen and look.
- Head out of shipping channels.
- Sound fog horn.
- Use echo sounder and all other aids to plot position.
- Have white flares at hand.

7. Tidal Heights

7.1

1)	C	5)	D
2)	B	6)	F
3)	A	7)	E
4)	G		

7.2

a) 12.2m
b) 14.9m
c) 7.7 −1.5 = 6.2m
d) Yes. 2.2m − 4.3m = Dries 2.1m
e) No. Depth at MHWN = 7.2m − 6.2m = 1m
f) Yes just!
At MHWS −0.5 = 8.8m, the mast just fouls the cable.
At drying height 6.4m + 2.0m = 8.4m, the keel touches the bottom.
A brave (or foolish) navigator could attempt it at a tidal height of 8.6m, which occurs shortly before and after MHWS.

7.3

Between about 1200 and 1400 and between 0000 and 0200 BST.

7.4

a)	0419	5.8m	b)	1502	6.4m	c)	0009	6.5m
	1149	1.7m		2224	0.8m		0802	0.9m

7.5

Height required: 2.0m drying height
          +1.2m draught
          ————
          3.2m

LW   0.8m   HW 1300 BST   6.7m   springs
From graph   HW − 2 hrs 40 mins
The yacht will float at 1020 hrs

7.6

HW   1919 BST   5.7m   LW 1.5m
2359 is HW + 4 hrs 40 mins
Height of tide   2.7m
Tide will fall   2.7 − 1.5 = 1.2m
Draught   +1.7m
                   ————
                   2.9m

Clearance = Depth − (tidal fall + draught) = 3.2m − 2.9m
                                  = 0.3m

Tidal Heights continued

7.7

Dover HW GMT	1323	6.1m	LW	2056	1.3m	
Corr. Dungeness	– 11	+ 0.8m		– 13	+0.2m	
Dungeness BST	1412	6.9m		2143	1.5m	

7.8

Dover HW GMT	0104	6.5m	LW	0.9m	HW	1326	6.5m
Corr. Richborough	+15	– 3.3m		– 0.8m		+15	–3.3m
Richborough BST	0219	3.2m		0.1m		1441	3.2m

From the graph, the height at + 5 hrs 21 mins is the same as at –3 hrs 24 mins. (Note that this transfer can only be done when the ranges of the two tides are the same.)
The yacht will refloat at 1441–3 hrs 24 mins = 1117
The height of the tide at this time is 0.7m.

7.9

HW Dover GMT	1538	6.1m	LW	1.4m	Range 4.7m
Corr. Margate	+ 44	– 1.7m		– 0.5m	
Margate BST	1722	4.4m		0.9m	

From graph   Height of tide at 2015 (HW + 2 hrs 53 mins)   =   3.2m
Tide will fall   3.2m – 0.9m =   2.3m
Minimum depth   =   2.3 fall of tide
                      +   1.7 draught
                      +   1.0 clearance
                      =   5.0m

7.10

a) High barometric pressure can depress tidal heights.

b) Low barometric pressure can result in tides higher than predicted. Storms cause surges giving exceptionally high tides particularly in estuaries, the North Sea coast and areas where the land funnels.

8. Tidal Streams

8.1

a) 042°(T) 2.4kn   b) 058°(T) 0.2kn   c) 230°(T) 1.3sp 0.7np Int 1.0kn

8.2

a) 260°(T) 1.8kn   b) 093°(T) 0.6kn

You can use a Breton plotter to measure the angle of the arrows.

8.3

3 May: HW Dover 1057 BST   Range 6.0m   Springs
Use the tidal stream chartlets to note that the stream is SW-going until 2½ hours before HW
ie 0830. It would therefore be wise to complete the passage in a wind with tide situation when the
sea will be flat enough for the motor cruiser. By 1030 there will be over 2½ knots of stream when
the passage would be very uncomfortable.

8.4

a) 31 August   ◇A HW – 2   HW 1301 BST   1031 – 1131   Springs   080°(T) 2.4kn

b) 8 August   ◇C HW + 3   HW 0521 BST   0751 – 0850   Neaps   248°(T) 1.0kn

c) 24 May   ◇B HW   HW 0231 BST   0201 – 0301   Range 4.6m Midway springs/neaps   066°(T) 0.8sp 0.4np Int 0.6kn

d) 9 June   ◇N HW +1   HW 1717 BST   1747 – 1847   Range 4.2m   018°(T) 3.9sp 2.2np Int 2.8kn

e) 21 June   ◇O HW – 2   HW 1413 BST   1143 – 1243   Range 5.2m   Slack

f) 9 August   ◇F HW – 1   HW 1857 BST   1727 – 1827   Range 2.9m   048°(T) 1.2sp 0.7np Ext 0.6kn

g) 6 May   ◇J HW – 4   HW 1324 BST   0854 – 0954   Range 6.4m   236°(T) 2.3sp 1.3np Ext 2.5kn

8.5

a) HW 0443 BST. Stream SW-going HW Dover + 4½ hrs. Stream SW-going from approx 0913.
b) HW 1717 BST. Stream slack 3 hrs before HW Dover. Stream becomes N-going at approx 1447.

Tidal Streams *continued*

8.6

The stream runs more slowly where it is shallow close to the shore particularly where the bottom shelves gradually as at Quend Plage. Tidal diamond ◇K◇ is situated in water of approximately 20m where the bottom is irregular. Streams inshore could be less than half the rate at ◇K◇ but will change direction earlier.

8.7

  a) Tidal stream atlas.
  b) Tidal diamonds.
  c) Tidal stream atlas.

9. Estimated Position

9.1

EP   50° 41'.7N   01°12'.0E

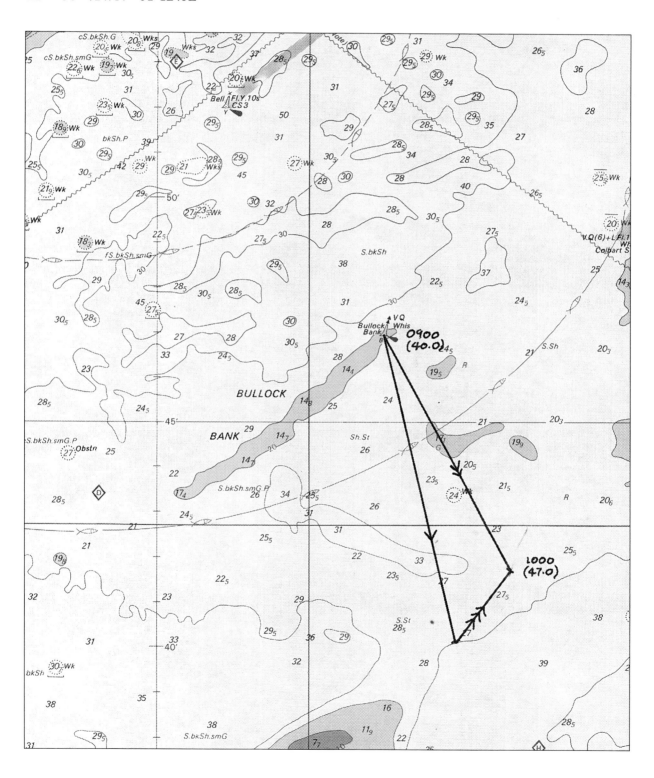

Estimated Position *continued*

9.2

Tidal stream   HW   1301BST   Springs

⟨K⟩   HW   1230–1330   020°(T)   1.6kn

EP   50° 25'.8N   01°23'.6E

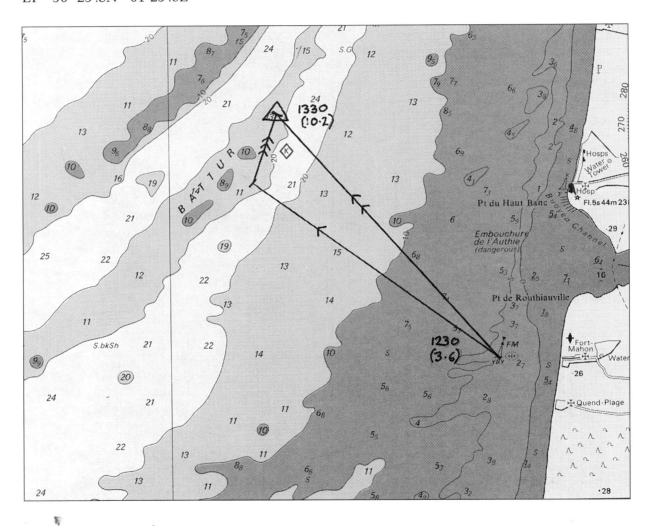

Estimated Position *continued*

9.3

Tidal streams	HW	1335BST	Springs	
F	HW–2	1105–1205	057°(T)	1.2kn
H	HW–1	1205–1305	032°(T)	1.0kn

EP   50° 37'.9N   01° 05'.7E
Charted depth 7.7m on Bassurelle Bank

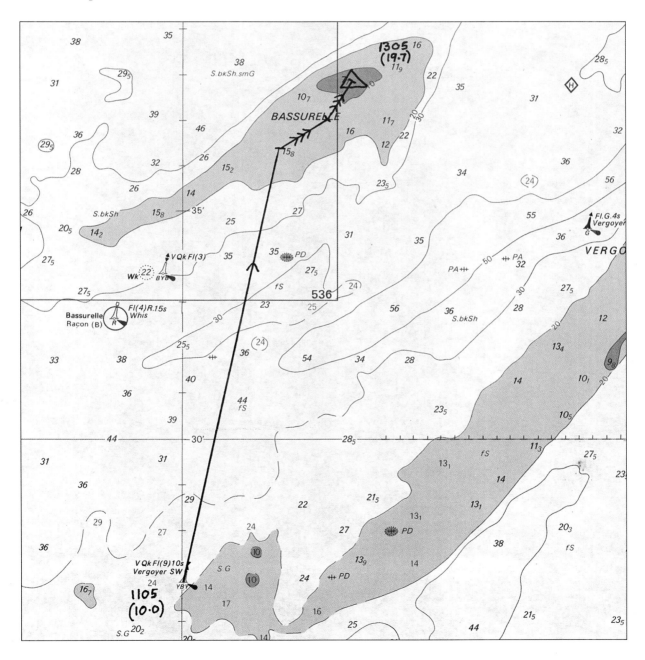

Estimated Position continued

9.4

Tidal streams   HW   0731BST   Neaps

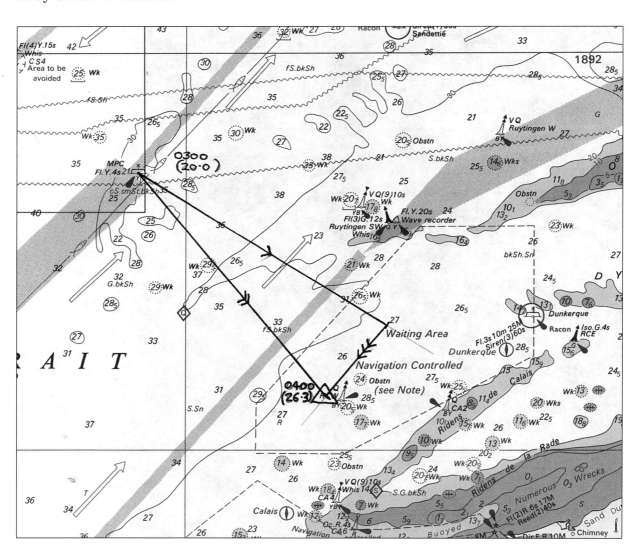

                 HW – 4   0301–0401   220°(T)   2.0kn

Course 135°(M)

$$\frac{-3°}{132°\text{(T)}}$$

$$\frac{-10° \text{ leeway}}{122°\text{(T)}}$$

EP 51° 01'.2N   01°44'.8E

Buoy is RCW N Cardinal

Estimated Position continued

9.5

Tidal streams	HW	0724 BST		Range 4.2m		
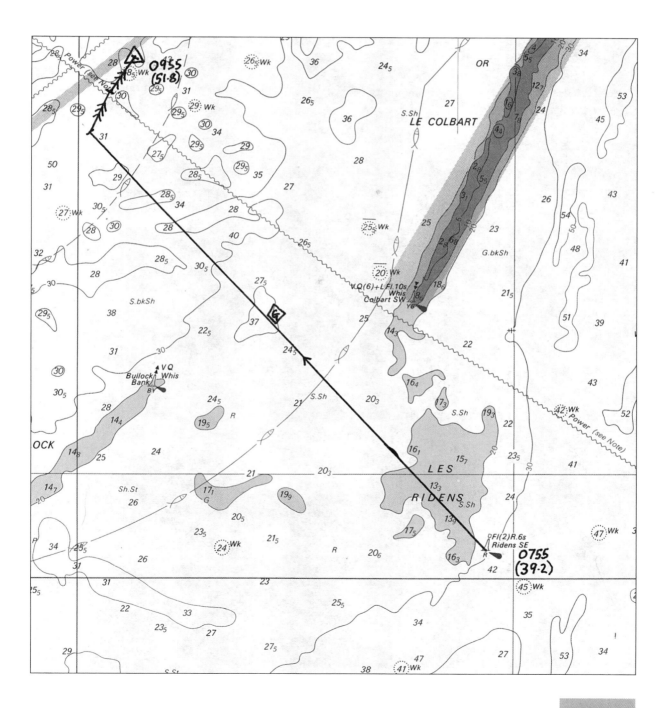 G	HW + 1	0755 – 0855	025°(T)	1.4sp	0.8np	Int 1.0
G	HW + 2	0855 – 0955	034°(T)	1.2sp	0.7np	Int 0.9

EP   50°54'.3N   01°07'.0E

Estimated Position continued

9.6

First course	135°(C)	Second course	200°(C)
	141°(M)	No leeway	202°(M)
	138°(T)		199°(T)
	+10° leeway		
	148°(T)		

Tidal streams   HW   0926   BST   Range   4.9m

◇P	HW – 3	0555–0655	230°(T)	2.6sp	1.5np	Int	2.2
◇Q	HW – 2	0655–0755	220°(T)	1.2sp	0.7np	Int	1.0

EP 50° 58'.2N   01° 34'.4E

Note that the heading of 138°(T) is at right angles to the Traffic Separation Scheme.

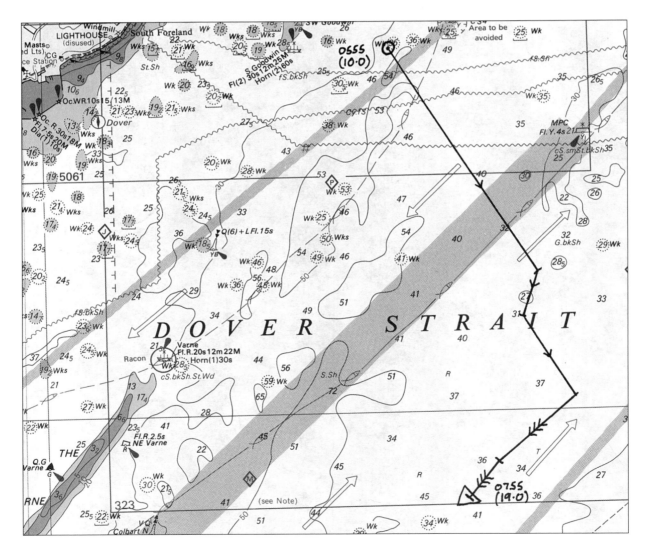

Estimated Position continued

9.7

Projected EP:	Course	110°(C)
		115°(M)
		112°(T)
	Leeway	+10°
		122°(T)

HW Dover 1352 BST. Range 5.1m

⟨J⟩ HW + 2   1522 – 1622   060°(T)   2.3sp   1.3np   Int   2.0

Draw line parallel to tide from point at which ground track meets Traffic Separation Scheme to water track. Measure logged distance along water track.
Log reads   21.8 + 3.9 = 25.7

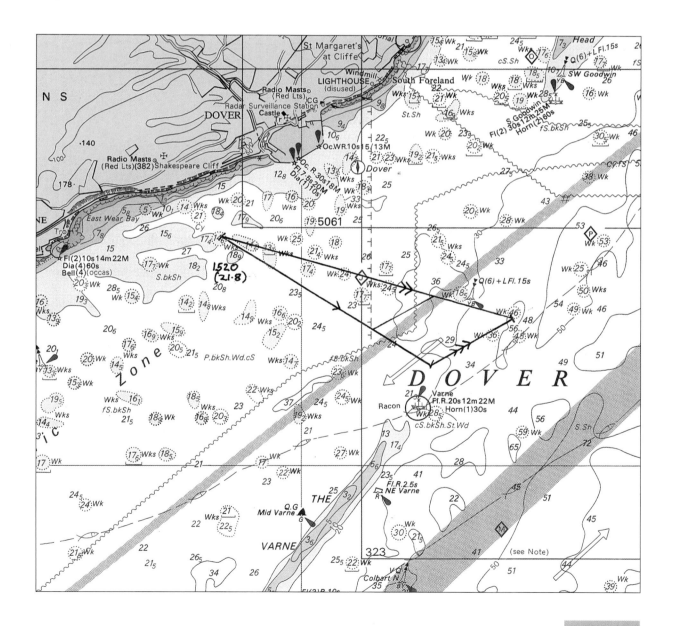

10. Buoyage and Lights

10.1

The broad arrow near the title of the chart shows the direction of SW to NE.

10.2

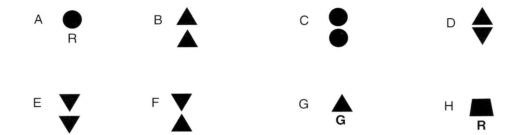

10.3

To starboard as it is a North Cardinal mark.

10.4

a) Port	b) Either side	c) Starboard	d) Either side
e) Starboard	f) Port	g) Starboard	

10.5

Flashing white every 10 seconds and fixed red.

10.6

No, the actual light would not be visible from the cockpit of a small yacht as the curvature of the earth would preclude this. The figure given (25M) is the nominal range, it assumes that the earth is flat and that the visibility is at least 10M.   From the Dipping Distance table:

Height of eye	2m
Height of light	31m
Max range	14.5M

10.7

a) Walde	b) Boulogne S breakwater	c) Cap d'Alprech
d) Calais W breakwater	e) Pointe de Lornel	f) Calais

11. Course to Steer

All times are given in BST.

11.1

a) 014°(T) + 3°W = 017°(M)
b) 4.6kn

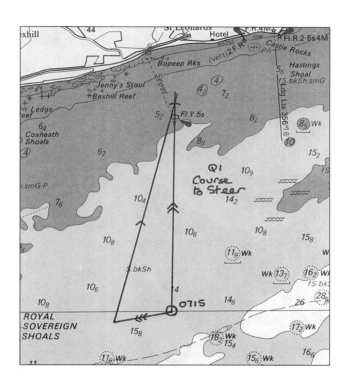

Course to Steer continued

11.2

HW 1300 BST. Springs.

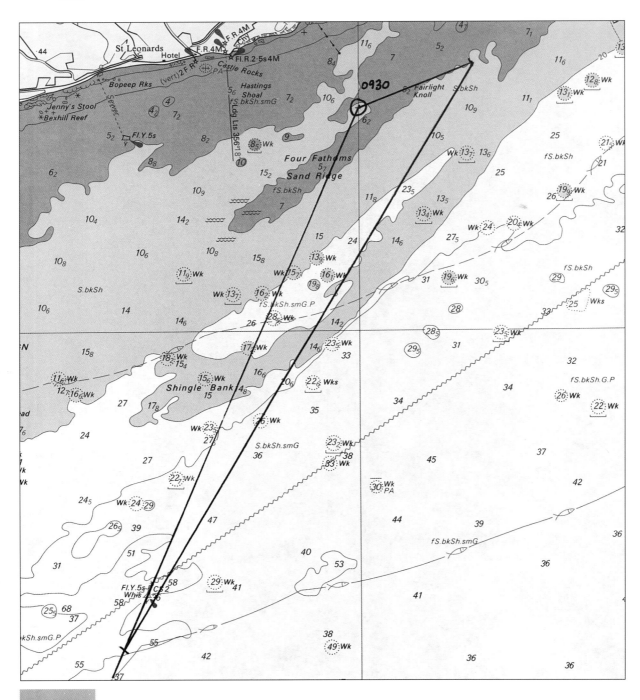 HW – 3   0930–1030   068°(T)   2.6kn

   a)   210°(T) = 213°(M)

   b)   13.1kn

   c)   Distance to travel ÷ Speed over ground x 60 = Passage time in minutes

$$\frac{11.8}{13.1} \text{ x } 60 = 54 \text{ mins} \quad \text{ETA} = 0930 + 54 \text{ mins} = 1024$$

Course to Steer continued

11.3

8 August: HW Dover 1745 BST. Range 3.4m. Neaps.

Ⓐ HW – 3 1415–1515 075°(T) 1.5kn

  a) 012°(T) = 015°(M)

  b) 5.4kn

See page 60 for chartwork.

11.4

7 May. HW Dover 1414 BST. Range 6.0m. Springs.

Ⓐ HW + 4 1745–1845 263°(T) 2.0kn

   HW + 5 1845–1945 263°(T) 1.8kn

CTS 349°(T) = 352°(M) + 4°W = 356°(C)

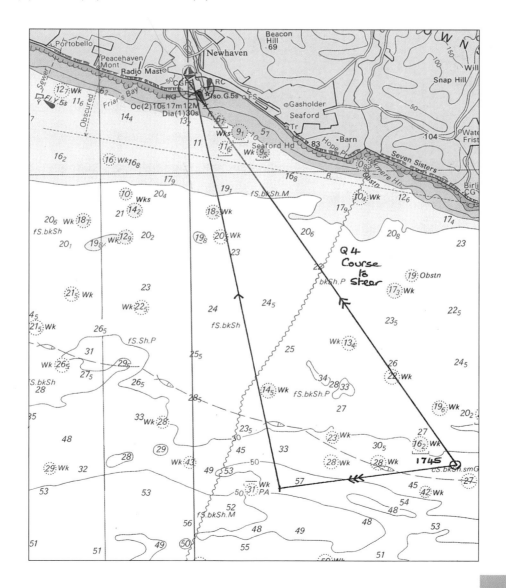

Course to Steer continued

11.5

30 May. HW 0855 BST. 6.0m. LW 1.3m. Range 4.7m.

⟨C⟩ HW + 3 1125–1225 248°(T) 1.8sp 1.0np Int 1.4kn ½ hr 0.7

CTS 194°(T) = 197°(M) –3°E = 194°(C)

11.6

16 July. HW 1137 6.2m LW 1.2m Range 5.0m.

⟨C⟩ HW–2 0907–1007 068°(T) 2.3sp 1.3np Int 1.9kn

a) CTS 142°(T) = 145°(M) – 6°E = 139°(C)
b) Distance 3.2M ÷ SOG 5.8kn x 60 = 33 mins = 0940
c) 145°(M) + 10° = 155°(M) – 5°E = 150°(C)

Note: The stream inshore would be less than at ⟨C⟩.
The tidal diamond has been used to give a definitive answer.

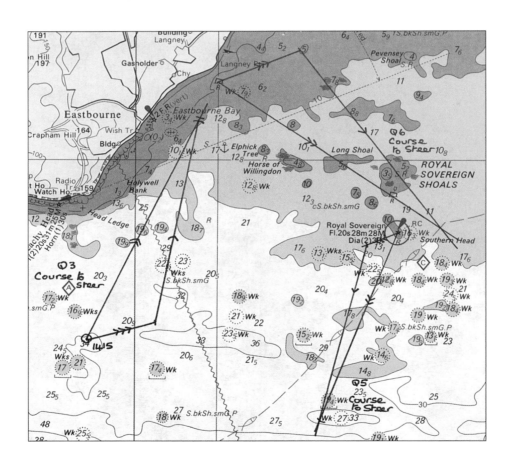

Course to Steer *continued*

11.7

26 July. HW 1918 BST. 5.8m. LW 1.8m. Range 4.0m.

⟨E⟩ HW – 5 1348–1448 211°(T) 2.1sp 1.2np Int 1.4kn.

a) Fix 50° 52'.9N 00° 56'.7E

Note: Two of the bearings cut at a narrow angle but the objects are close and can be positively identified. The cocked hat is almost non existent so accuracy is reasonable.

b) CTS 294°(T) = 297°(M) – 10° Leeway = 287°(M)
   287°(M) + 5°W Deviation = 292°(C)

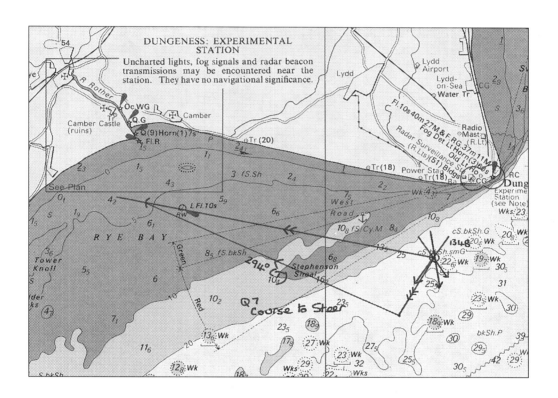

12. Navigational Instruments

12.1

a) ● GPS gives worldwide coverage.
   ● Unaffected by geographical features.
   ● No errors caused by position in the lattice.
   ● Less effect from atmospheric conditions (except lightning).
   ● Likely to be a long-term system.

b) Disadvantage: primarily a military system which may be altered or switched off by the USA.

12.2

a) A position fixing instrument such as Decca or GPS can be programmed with waypoints ie with latitudes and longitudes of positions where the course will change, such as buoys and off headlands. A digital display will inform the navigator of the bearing and distance of the waypoint from the yacht's present position. Some navigators waypoint the centre of the compass rose on the chart which allows a quick and simple plot of the yacht's position.

b) The computer in most electronic navigation units knows the direct track from one waypoint to the next or from a defined position to a pre-entered destination. At any time it can tell the navigator if the yacht is off track. It will also advise as to which side of the track she is currently situated and which way to steer to bring her back on line to correct her cross track error.

12.3

It is quicker to shape a course. By following the rhumb line you will spend a significant part of the passage pointing slightly into the tide. On a 12 hour passage the tidal stream effect as predicted on a course to steer should sweep you off the line and then back to it, allowing the yacht to make the passage with minimal reduction in speed because of the tide.

12.4

The MOB function will bring you back to the geographical position where the man fell. You should now start to search in the direction the tidal stream is flowing. If the man is not immediately recovered, send a Mayday call.

12.5

The Dutchman's log involves dropping a chip of wood overboard at the bow and timing how long it takes to reach the stem. A nautical mile is 6080 feet.

13. Pilotage

13.1

To port.

13.2

a) Dover: keep clear of the entrance you are approaching.
b) Rye: more than 3m over the bar.
c) Folkestone: port closed. Ferry sailing in 15 minutes.
d) Boulogne: sluicing from River Liane.

13.3

Enter close to RH side of entrance. Fl (2 + 1) 15s, to avoid ships entering harbour.
- Listen on VHF channel 12.
- When light is abeam turn to 136°(M) to find FR and FG. Slow down until these are identified against background light clutter.
- When FR at entrance bears 126°(M) a second FR should be in transit behind.
- Follow transit – keep on starboard side.
- Leave FG to starboard then 3FG (triangle) to starboard before entering Marina. Yachts moor to pontoon on starboard side.
- Observe traffic signals from control tower.

13.4

A back bearing of less than 200°(M) on Cap Gris Nez Lighthouse will clear the wreck to seaward and a bearing of no less than 163°(M) on Tardinghen Belfry will ensure that it is safe to come into the shallower water in order to cheat the tidal stream. Once CA3 Buoy is identified, a subsequent clearing bearing will ensure clearance on the wrecks close to CA1 Buoy. Pass close to CA3 to avoid the 1.3m charted depth. Once abeam CA3, hug the coast in 5m water.

13.5

Select a safe cruising speed of perhaps 7 or 8 knots and steer 340°(M) to a point downtide of Newhaven. When the 5m contour is reached, turn on to 105°(M) and motor eastwards watching the echo sounder closely.

This approach into the tide will give good control over ground speed on the final run towards the pier. The fog signal on the breakwater will indicate the entrance.

An alternative is to head approximately 2½ M to the east of Newhaven and run down with the tide to the entrance, still using the depth contours.

Pilotage continued

13.6

Log reading	Elapsed time (mins)	Course	Notes
0.0		158°(M)	Log to zero. Depart Sandettie LV.
4.6	13.8	158°(M)	Depth 13m (reduced to soundings) **Alter course 213°(M)**
6.1	18.3	213°(M)	Abeam Dunkerque Lanby 1.8M to port.
8.9	26.7	213°(M)	Abeam CA2 North Cardinal 1.25M to port.
12.2	36.3	213°(M)	CA4 West Cardinal buoy approx 2 cables to port. **Alter course 098°(M).** Careful watch for commercial traffic.
13.0	39.0	098°(M)	CA6 (port lateral) 2.5 cables to starboard.
16.8	50.4	098°(M)	Calais breakwater ahead. Slow to speed limit. Signals = at least 3 lights = NO ENTRY Close watch for ferry traffic.

Pilotage continued

13.6

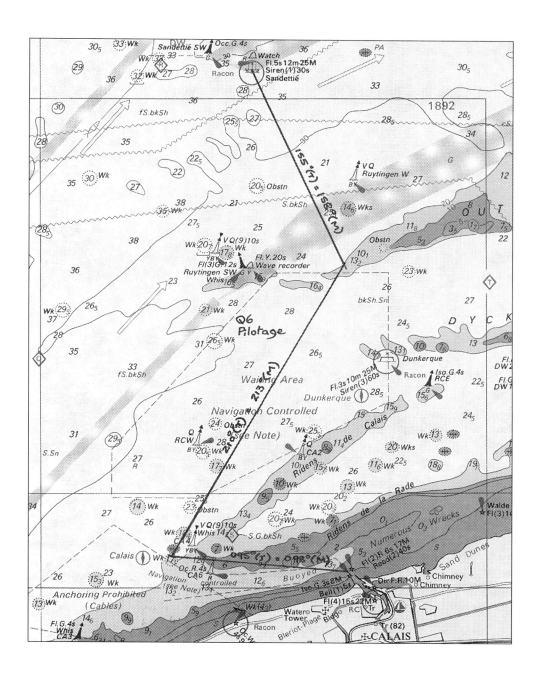

14. Meteorology

14.1

a) Visibility of less than 1100 yards (1000 metres).
b) A clockwise change in wind direction.
c) Pressure change of 1.6 to 3.5 millibars in the last three hours.
d) System moving at 15 to 25 knots.
e) After 12 hours from the time of issue.
f) Visibility of 2 to 5 nautical miles.
g) Nothing significant ie no showers, rain, mist.
h) Within 6 hours from the time of issue of the warning.

14.2

a) F4   b) F7

14.3

Buys Ballot's Law states, 'If you stand with your back to the wind in the northern hemisphere, low pressure will be on your left hand and high pressure on your right.'

14.4

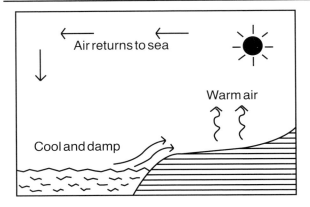

14.5

Sea fog (advection fog) forms when damp tropical maritime air is cooled as it blows over a cold surface. In the spring and early summer warm tropical air comes in from the warmer south but the sea remains cold until later in the summer. Sea fog occurs most frequently in winds of Beaufort F2 to F4 but can, on occasions, persist in winds of F5 or even F6. A change to a colder airstream will disperse this type of fog or stronger winds will lift it off the surface to simulate low stratus cloud.

14.6

As the wind has been blowing strongly in one direction for a few days a consistent wave pattern will have become established. A sudden windshift will cause confused seas and possibly dangerously high 'pyramid' waves. The weather is also likely to be squally.

Meteorology *continued*

14.7

a) Humber: High cirrus cloud with a possible halo around the sun. The cloud will gradually thicken and become lower as the warm front approaches.
West Sole: Good visibility with a few cumulus causing showers.

b) As the warm front approaches Dover, the cloud cover will become lower. As the front passes the rain and increasing humidity will cause poor visibility and there may be fog in the warm sector. When the cold front passes there will be a marked improvement in the visibility.

c) Thames and Humber will be south of the depression. Irish Sea will be north of the depression.

d) Shelter from the east and north are required.

e) Plymouth: The passage of the cold front will cause the wind to veer, the visibility to improve and the rain to become showery.
Lundy and Fastnet: The cyclonic wind occurs near the centre of the low. The isobars are close together therefore the wind will be strong. As the low moves east the wind becomes northerly.

15. Passage Planning

15.1

a) 34M approx 3½ hours.
b) HW Rye is 1100. Access 2 hours before and 3 hours after HW 0900 to 1400.
c) Newhaven Marina access 5 hours before to 5 hours after HW.
   HW Newhaven is 1100 BST. Access 0600–1600.
d) 0530–1300.
e) ETA at 1000 with last of flood tide is preferable. ETD is therefore 0630.
f) (i) Overfalls. Take a clearing bearing of not greater than 090°(M) on Royal Sovereign.
   (ii) Shoals and overfalls. Once clear of Holywell Bank take a back bearing of 252°(M) on Beachy Head.
g) Fix the position of the yacht and work out the bearing on the chart. Using a GPS receiver, enter the entrance as a waypoint. The instrument will then display bearing and distance.

15.2

a) 44M, 9 hours approx.
b) Yes, the wind is offshore.
c) The channel is unlit. You should enter in daylight at 1130.
d) HW Rye is 0015 BST Sunday 30 August. Depart just after HW, say 0030. You may arrive slightly early and have to anchor or heave-to in the lee near Pte du Haut Banc to wait for the tide to rise.
e) You will be departing at night. Keep in the white occulting sector of the leading light.
f) Shipping is likely to be busy to the SW of the Traffic Separation Scheme. The shallow area of Vergoyer bank should be avoided. Groffliers is shallow and should be entered with care.

15.3

a) 0615, 0745 and 0815.
b) 26M (crossing the Traffic Separation Scheme at 90°). 5½ hours.
c) Folkestone HW 1930: accessible 1630–2230.
d) i) 1145–1730
   ii) 0545–1145 and 1730–2330
e) You should leave the Bassin de L'Ouest at 0815. To save a long passage against the tidal stream you could wait at the moorings outside the lock until about midday then make the passage to Folkestone. With a favourable stream you can head across the TSS at 90° and be set on to a ground track close to the rhumb line. ETD1200, ETA1730.
f) ● The Traffic Separation Scheme must be crossed at 90°.
   ● Very busy shipping lane.
   ● Ferries at Calais and Folkestone and out of Dover.
   ● Varne ridge.
g) Listen on VHF dual watch to channels 16 and 22.
   Blue flag is hoisted on S arm of harbour 15 mins before ferry sails.

Passage Planning *continued*

15.4

A low pressure system is approaching. The wind is likely to veer and could strengthen from the west making Le Touquet uncomfortable or untenable. Your best option is to divert to Boulogne which is well sheltered and convince the crew the restaurants are better there.

15.5

a) (i) 60M rhumb line
(ii) 70–80M tacking
b) You should depart on port tack to be on the English side in time for the veer. This would also put you in the lee when the wind freshens.
c) You should cross the Channel with a W-going tidal stream (W-going 0400–0745). Leave at 0400. Tack on to starboard in Rye Bay and keep in shallow water while the tide is foul.
d) Approximate ETA 1800 hours. Newhaven Marina opens 1930.

15.6

a) 77M.
b) It would be unwise to attempt the passage without refuelling on the way. The best port at which to refuel is Dover which is close and accessible at all times.
c) Tidal streams off Calais   NE 0900–1445
Dover to Newhaven   SW 1445–1730
Depart Calais at 0900 and make passage across the Straits, wind against tide, to Dover (22M) arriving about 1100. Refuel and depart as soon as the tidal stream slackens at about 1400 to make the 58M passage in just over 3 hours, arriving about 1700.

16. Passage Making

16.1

a) Approximately 41M (crossing the Traffic Separation Scheme from ZC2 area).

b) 28 June: HW Dover 0827 BST.
Stream fair to Cap Gris Nez: HW – 2½ hrs to HW + 3½ hrs.
0600 to 1200.

c) *Etaples*   HW same as Dover = 0827 BST.
Access HW–2 to HW+2 = 0627 to 1027.
Leave at HW–2 to be off Le Touquet at best time ie HW–1 = 0730.

Dover Access to Wellington Dock = HW –1½ to HW+1
There is a waiting pontoon in deep sheltered water so this time is not critical.

d) ▪ Ferry traffic and fishing boats entering Boulogne.
▪ Traffic in Traffic Separation Scheme.
▪ Inshore traffic from Boulogne to Cap Gris Nez and on the English coast.
▪ Commercial traffic in Dover.
▪ Strong tide across entrance.
▪ Wreck inside W entrance.

Passage Making *continued*

16.2

28 June. Running fix.
Course 005°(C) – 4°W = 001°(M) = 358°(T)
Distance 2.7M.

HW 0827 BST 5.9m. LW 1.5m. Range 4.4m
⟨L⟩ HW   0757–0857 007°(T) 1.7sp 1.0np   Int 1.3kn ½hr 0.65
Fix. 50° 40'.1N   01° 31'.0E

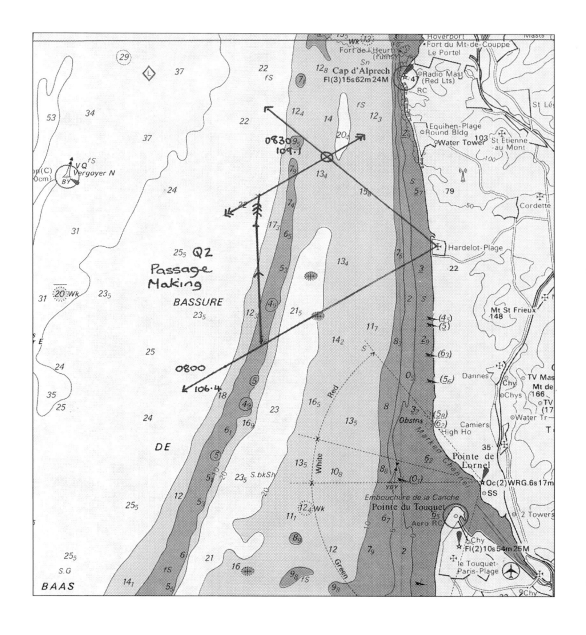

Passage Making continued

16.3 ▶

Fix. 50° 45'.8N 01° 33'.1E

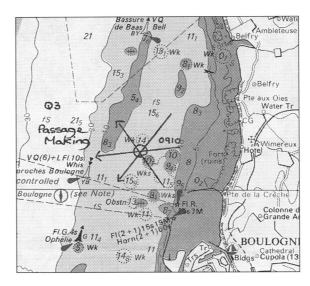

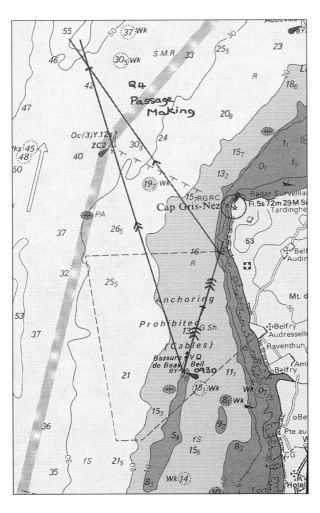

◀ **16.4**

HW 0827 BST Range 4.4m.

◇Ⓝ HW + 1   0857–0957 018°(T) 3.9sp 2.2np Int 2.9kn ½ hr 1.45

◇Ⓝ HW + 2   0957–1057 018°(T) 3.3sp 2.0np Int 2.6kn ½ hr 1.3

  a) CTS 327°(T) = 330°(M) + 5°W = 335°(C)
  b) Distance 5.2M.   SOG 7.1kn = 44 mins = 1014

Passage Making continued

16.5

Course	322°(C)
Deviation	– 6°W
Magnetic	316°(M)
Leeway	+5°
Magnetic	321°(M)
Variation	– 3°W
	318°(T)

◇M HW + 3   1057–1157   033°(T) 1.7sp 0.9np Int 1.2kn
EP at 1200 51° 02'.3N 01° 23'.9E

The yacht will pass to the east of Varne Light Vessel.

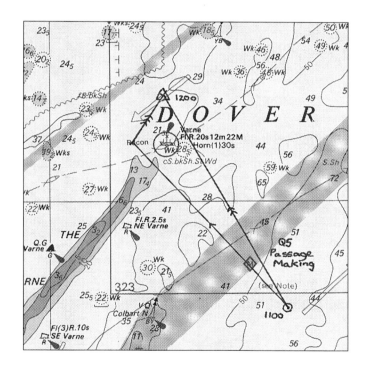

Part III

EXTRACTS

NEWHAVEN
E. Sussex

CHARTS
Admiralty 2154, 1652; Stanford 9; Imray C9; OS 198
TIDES
0004 Dover; ML 3·6; Duration 0550; Zone 0 (GMT).

Standard Port SHOREHAM

Times				Height (metres)			
HW		LW		MHWS	MHWN	WLWN	MLWS
0500	1000	0000	0600	6·3	4·9	2·0	0·6
1700	2200	1200	1800				

Differences NEWHAVEN

−0015	−0010	0000	0000	+0·4	+0·2	0·0	−0·2

EASTBOURNE

−0010	−0005	+0015	+0020	+1·1	+0·6	+0·2	+0·1

SHELTER
Good, but with strong on-shore winds there is often a difficult sea at the entrance. Accessible in all weathers but with strong on-shore winds pass close to breakwater; there are heavy breaking seas on E side of dredged channel.
NAVIGATION
Waypoint 50°46'·20N 00°03'·70E, 168°/348° from/to West breakwater Lt, 0·32M. Harbour silts up and dredging is in continuous operation. Cargo vessels and ferries often warp off by means of hawsers run across the harbour.
LIGHTS AND MARKS
Traffic signals, displayed from Tr on W side of river.
Triangle over ball, or G Lt – only entry permitted.
Ball over triangle, or R Lt – only departure permitted.
Ball, triangle, ball (vert) or
    RGR Lts (vert) – No entry or departure
Ball or G R Lts (vert) – Entry and departure permitted with care for vessels under 15m

Swing bridge signals
FIG – Bridge opening or closing
FR – Vessels may pass N to S
FG – Vessels may pass S to N
RADIO TELEPHONE
VHF Ch 16; 12 (H24). Newhaven Marina Ch 80 M.
TELEPHONE (0273)
Hr Mr 514131; MRSC Lee-on-Solent 552100; Harbour Signal Station 514131 ext. 247; # (0703) 827350; Marinecall 0898 500 456; Police 515801; Dr 515076; Ⓗ 609411 (Accidents (0273) 696955).

FACILITIES
EC Wednesday; **Newhaven Marina** (300+50 visitors) ☎ 513881, Slip, FW, ME, El, Sh, AC, BH (18 ton), C (10 ton), CH, V, R, Bar, Gas, Gaz, Ⓠ (Access HW ∓ 5), fuel pontoon 200 yds N of ent; **Newhaven Marina YC** ☎ 513976; **Sealink Quays** ☎ 514131, Slip P, D, L, FW, ME, El, Sh, C (3 ton), CH, AB, V, R, Bar; **Ship and Industrial Repairs** ☎ 516298, ME, El, Sh, C; **Cantell & Son** ☎ 514118, ME, Sh , CH, SM, Slip, C, ACA; **Golden Arrow Marine** ☎ 513987, ME; **Newhaven and Seaford SC** ☎ Seaford 890077, M, FW; **Newhaven YC** ☎ 513770, Slip, M, P, D, ME, El, Sh, CH, AB; **Meeching Boats** (80) ☎ 514907, ME, El, Sh; **Russell Simpson Marine** ☎ 513458 CH, El; **Leonard Marine** ☎ 515987 BY, El, ME, Sh, Slip, SM; **C & E Sports** ☎ 515450, Gas; **L D Electronics** ☎ 56179, Ⓔ; **Nautical Electronic Services** ☎ 693258, Ⓔ.
Town P, V, R, Bar. ▫ ; Ⓑ ; ⇌ ; ✈ (Shoreham).

FOLKESTONE
Kent

CHARTS
Admiralty 1991, 1892; Stanford 9; Imray C8; OS 179
TIDES
−0010 Dover; ML 3·7; Duration 0500; Zone 0 (GMT).

Standard Port DOVER

Times				Height (metres)			
HW		LW		MHWS	MHWN	MLWN	MLWS
0000	0600	0100	0700	6·7	5·3	2·0	0·8
1200	1800	1300	1900				

Differences FOLKESTONE

−0020	−0005	−0010	−0010	+0·4	+0·4	0·0	−0·1

DUNGENESS

−0010	−0015	−0020	−0010	+1·0	+0·6	+0·4	+0·1

SHELTER
Good shelter except in strong E winds.
NAVIGATION
Waypoint 51°04'·30N 01°12'·00E, 150°/330° from/to breakwater head Lt, 0·26M. Beware Copt Rocks and Mole Head Rocks. Also ferries and pulling off wires from the jetty.
LIGHTS AND MARKS
Ldg Lts 295° at ferry terminal, FR and FG (occas). 305° on QG Lt at E pierhead leads to inner harbour. Bu flag or 3FR(vert) at FS on S arm, ¼hr before ferry sails, indicates port closed.
RADIO TELEPHONE
VHF Ch 16; 22 (occas).
TELEPHONE (0303)
Hr Mr 54947; MRCC Dover 210008; # (0304) 202441; Marinecall 0898 500 456; Police 850055; Port Health Office 57574; Ⓗ 57311.
FACILITIES
EC Wednesday (larger shops open all day); **South Quay BR Slipway** Slip (free), FW; **Folkestone Y and MB Club** ☎ 51574, Bar, D, FW, L, Slip, M; **Sealink C** (by arrangement 5 ton); **Garage** P and D (100 yds, cans); **Bosun's Locker** ☎ 55752, CH. Town P, V, R, Bar. ▫ ; Ⓑ ; ⇌ ; ✈ (Lydd). A marina is under construction

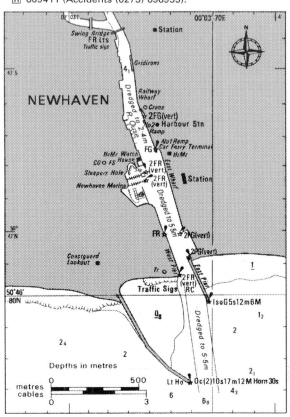

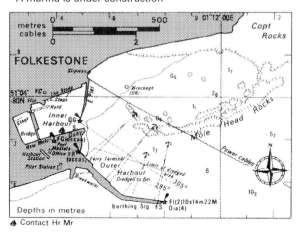

RYE
E. Sussex

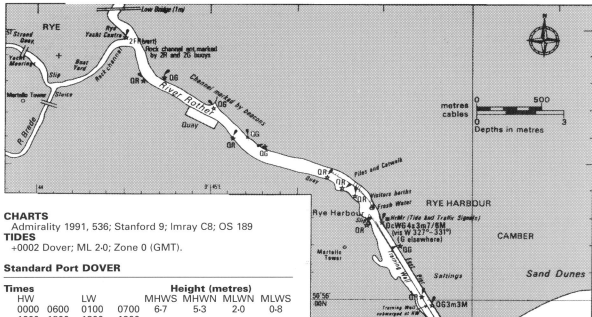

CHARTS
Admirality 1991, 536; Stanford 9; Imray C8; OS 189
TIDES
+0002 Dover; ML 2·0; Zone 0 (GMT).

Standard Port DOVER

Times				Height (metres)			
HW		LW		MHWS	MHWN	MLWN	MLWS
0000	0600	0100	0700	6·7	5·3	2·0	0·8
1200	1800	1300	1900				

Differences RYE HARBOUR						
+0005	−0010	No data		−1·4	−1·7	Dries
RYE (approaches)						
+0005	−0010	No data		+1·0	+0·7	+0·2	+0·1
HASTINGS						
0000	−0010	−0030	−0030	+0·8	+0·5	+0·1	−0·1

SHELTER
Very good in river. Entrance requires care when wind strong (force 7 or over) from SE to SW. Enter HW-2 to HW + 3. Rye harbour is ¾M inside entrance and is a small village used by commercial shipping. The town of Rye is another 2M up river; it is a Cinque Port.
NAVIGATION
Waypoint Rye Fairway (safe water) buoy, LFl 10s, 50°54'·00N 00°48'·13E, 150°/330° from/to West Arm head Lt, 1·81M. Beware:
(1) Narrow entrance. Limited width of channel (42m).
(2) Bar at entrance.
(3) Strong flood stream in river – up to 4.5 kn (max HW −3 to HW −1).
(4) Shallow water E & W of entrance with ground swell or surf.
Harbour speed limit 6 kn.
LIGHTS AND MARKS
East Arm, head Q(9) 15s 9m 5M; Horn 7s.
Tide Signals on Hr Mr office:–
Night – FG 2·1-3·0m on bar
         F Purple Over 3·0m on bar
Day – None, but horizontal timbers on tripod beacon marking W arm indicate depths 5', 10' and 15'.
Traffic signals on Hr Mr office to indicate big ship movements
1 B Ball – Vessel entering
2 B Balls (hor) – Vessel leaving
3 B Balls (triangle) – Vessels entering and leaving.
In addtiion a Q orange Lt is exhibited at Harbour office.
RADIO TELEPHONE
VHF Ch 16; 14 (0900–1700 LT).
TELEPHONE (0797)
Hr Mr 225225; MRCC Dover 210008; # (0703) 223110; Marinecall 0898 500 456; Police 222112; Dr 222031; Ⓗ 222109.

FACILITIES
EC Tuesday; **Admiralty Jetty** Slip, M*, L, FW, AB*; **Strand Quay** Slip, M*, P and D (50m, cans), L, FW, AB*; **Rye Yacht Centre** ☎ 223336, M, L, FW, ME, EI, C (15 ton), AB; **Phillips BY** ☎ 223234, Slip, M, L, FW, ME, EI, C (3 ton); **Sandrock Marine** ☎ 222679, Slip, M, D, L, FW, ME, EI, CH, AB; **Sea Cruisers** ☎ 222070, ME, Sh, CH, ACA, **Town** ⊠; Ⓑ; ✈; ✈ (Lydd).
* See Hr Mr.

DOVER
Kent

CHARTS
Admiralty 1698, 1828, 1892; Stanford 1, 9, 19; Imray C8; OS 179

TIDES
0000 Dover; ML 3·7; Duration 0505; Zone 0 (GMT)

Standard Port DOVER

Times				Height (metres)			
HW		LW		MHWS	MHWN	MLWN	MLWS
0000	0600	0100		0700 6·7	5·3	2·0	0·8
1200	1800	1300	1900				

Differences DEAL
+0010 +0020 +0010 +0005 −0·6 −0·3 0·0 −0·0

RICHBOROUGH
+0015 +0015 +0030 +0030 −3·4 −2·6 −1·7 −0·7

MARGATE
+0050 −0040 −0010 +0030 −1·9 −1·4 −0·6 −0·3

SHELTER
The small craft anchorage is exposed to winds from NE through S to SW and in gales a heavy sea builds up. Visiting yachts are welcome for up to 14 days. For longer periods, apply in advance. Berthing instructions for Wellington Dock given from Dockmaster's Office at entrance to Granville Dock. Dock gates open, a minimum of HW − 1½ to HW + 1. Waiting pontoon available. Yachtsmen intending to leave the dock should inform the Dockmaster's Office (manned from HW −2). Small craft may not be left unattended in Outer Harbour.

NAVIGATION
Waypoint from SW 51°06'·15N 01°19'·77E, 180°/000° from/to Admiralty Pier Lt Ho, 0·5M. Waypoint from NE 51°07'·27N 01°21'·51E, 090°/270° from/to S end Eastern Arm, 0·5M. Frequent ferry and hovercraft movements through both entrances. Strong tides across entrances and high walls make entry under sail slow and difficult – use of engine very strongly recommended. Observe traffic signals and follow instructions of harbour patrol launch. Do not pass between buoy marking wreck inside W entrance, Q, and southern breakwater.

LIGHTS AND MARKS
Admiralty Pier head Fl 7·5s 21m 20M; W Tr; vis 096°–090°
International Port Traffic Signals are in operation, (see 6.2.7) shown for the Eastern entrance, day and night, on panels near Port Control; for Western entrance, day and night, on panels near Admiralty Pier Signal Station.
N.B. Specific permission to enter or leave Eastern or Western entrance *must* first be obtained from Port Control on VHF Ch 74, Ch 12 or, if not fitted with VHF/RT, with Aldis Lamp signals:
SV – I wish to enter port
SW – I wish to leave port.
Port Control will reply 'OK' or 'Wait'.
A Q Fl lamp from the Control Tower means keep clear of entrance you are approaching.

Docking signals
International Port Traffic Signals together with small Fl Y light to be shown 5 min before bridge is swung.

RADIO TELEPHONE
Call: *Dover Port Control* VHF Ch 16 **74**; 12 (H24). Channel Navigation Information Service (CNIS) – call: *Dover Coastguard* Ch 16 **69**; 11 **69** (Ch 80 for yachts). Information broadcasts on Ch 11 at H + 40, and also at H + 55 when visibility is less than 2M.

TELEPHONE (0304)
Hr Mr 240400; MRCC 210008; # (0304) 202411; Marinecall 0898 500 456; Police 240055; Ⓗ 201624

FACILITIES
EC Wednesday; **Wellington Dock** ☎ 240400 ext 4531, Slip, L, FW, C, AB; **Royal Cinque Ports YC** ☎ 206262, L, Bar, M, C, FW, R; **Dover Yacht Co** ☎ 201073, D, FW, ME, EI, Sh, C; **Dover Marine Supplies** ☎ 201677, D, FW, ME, EI, Sh, Slip, C, SM, ACA, CH; **Smye-Enright** ☎ 206295 CH;
Town P and D (cans), V, R, Bar. ▣; Ⓑ; ⇌; ✈ (Lydd).
Note: *A Yachtsman's Guide* is available from Harbour House or Dockmaster.

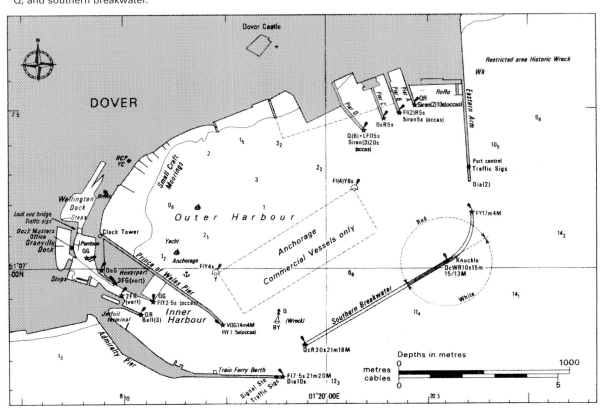

CALAIS
Pas de Calais

CHARTS
Admiralty 1352, 1892; SHOM 6474, 6651, 6681; ECM 1010; Stanford 1, 19, Imray C8

TIDES
Dover +0048; ML 4·1; Duration 0525; Zone –0100

Standard Port DIEPPE

Times				Height (metres)			
HW		LW		MHWS	MHWN	WLWN	MLWS
0100	0600	0100	0700	9·3	7·2	2·5	0·7
1300	1800	1300	1900				

Differences CALAIS

+0043	+0057	+0105	+0054	–2·2	–1·3	–0·5	+0·2

SHELTER
Shelter is very good especially in the marina. Bar is dredged to 4·5m but is liable to build up in heavy weather. Entrance is difficult in strong NW to NE winds. Enter Bassin Carnot if headed for the French canals otherwise use Bassin de l'Ouest, the marina.

NAVIGATION
Waypoint 50°58'·50N 01°49'·90E, 298°/118° from/to Jetée Ouest Lt, 0·43M. Entrance is relatively easy but beware the Ridens de la Rade, about 1 M N of entrance, a sandbank which shoals in places to about 0·75m and seas break on it. Entrance is well marked but there is a great deal of shipping, including ferries, which can be hazardous. Yachts are required to enter/leave under power. It is forbidden to tack in entrance channel.

LIGHTS and MARKS
From a point ¼M SE of CA 10 buoy, Fl(2) R 6s, the main Lt Ho, Fl(4) 15s, bearing 140° leads through entrance. Normal entry signals with following additions.
R Lt = indicates ferry leaving   movements
G Lt = ferry entering   prohibited
Lights on Tr of Gare Maritime are for car ferries and cargo vessels only. Yachts may not enter or leave when at least three Lts are on. They may follow a car ferry entering or leaving but must keep to the stbd side of the fairway. One R Lt denotes the presence of a dredger and does not mean movement is forbidden.
Bassin Carnot
Lock signals, gates open HW – 1½ to HW +¾.

2 G Lt hor	=	entry from Arrière Port permitted.
2 R Lt hor	=	entry from Arrière Port prohibited.
1 G Lt	=	entry from basin to Arrière Port permitted.
1 R Lt	=	entry from basin to Arrière Port prohibited.
2 blasts	=	request permission to enter Bassin Carnot.
4 blasts	=	request permission to enter Bassin de l'Ouest.

Bassin de l'Ouest
Or Lt = 10 mins before opening of lock.
R Lt   = All movement prohibited.
G Lt   = Movement authorised.
Dock gates and bridge open HW –1½, HW and HW + ½ (Sat and Sun HW–2 and HW+1).

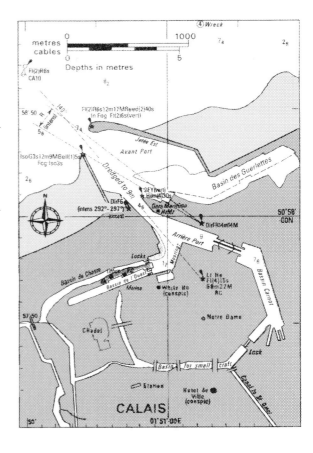

CALAIS

RADIOTELEPHONE
VHF Ch 12 16 (H24). Hoverport Ch 20 (occas). Carnot Lock Ch 12 (occas). Cap Gris Nez, Channel Navigation Information Service (CNIS), call: *Gris Nez Traffic* Ch 69 (H24). Information broadcasts in English and French on Ch 11, at H + 10, and also at H + 25 when visibility is less than 2 M.

TELEPHONE
Hr Mr 21.96.31.20; Aff Mar 21.34.52.70; Pilot (Quai de la Gare Maritime) 21.96.40.18; CROSS 21.87.21.87; SNSM 21.96.40.18; Port de Plaisance 21.34.55.23; Customs 21.34.75.40; Meteo 21.31.52.23; Auto 21.33.82.55; Dr 21.96.31.20; Hosp 21.97.99.60; Brit Consul 21.96.33.76.

FACILITIES
Marina (135 + 100 visitors) Tel. 21.34.55.23, D, FW, C (6 ton), BH (3 ton), AC, CH, Gaz, R, Lau, Sh, SM, V, Bar; Access HW – 1½ to HW + ½. **Bassin Du Paradis** AB, Grid; **The Calais YC** Tel. 21.34.60.00, M, P, Bar; **Chantiers Navals** Tel. 21.34.30.40, Sh; **Nautic Sport** Tel. 21.36.41.03, ME, EI, CH; **Godin Moteurs** Tel. 21.96.29.97, ME; **Marinerie** Tel. 21.34.47.83, CH. **Town** CH, V, Gaz, R, Bar. PO; Bank; Rly. Air.
Ferry UK – Dover.

BOULOGNE-SUR-MER
Pas de Calais

CHARTS
Admiralty 438, 1892, 2451; SHOM 6436, 6682, 6795; ECM 1010, 1011; Stanford 1, 9; Imray C31, C8
TIDES
Dover 0000; ML 5·0; Duration 0515; Zone −0100

Standard Port DIEPPE

Times				Height (metres)			
HW		LW		MHWS	MHWN	MLWN	MLWS
0100	0600	0100	0700	9·3	7·2	2·6	0·7
1300	1800	1300	1900				

Differences BOULOGNE
+0015	+0026	+0037	+0036	−1·8	−0·9	−0·5	+0·5

SHELTER
Good except in strong NE winds. Turbulent water when R Liane in spate; proceed with great care. Entrance possible in most weathers and at any state of tide. Yachts secure to pontoons in SW side of tidal basin alongside Quai Chanzy. Max length 10m (over 10m apply before arrival). Yacht berths tend to silt up.
NAVIGATION
Waypoint 50°44'·50N 01°33'·00E, 270°/090° from/to Digue Carnot Lt, 0·72M. Very busy commerical passenger and fishing port. Respect warnings and instructions given by harbour lights. There are no navigational dangers and entrance is easily identified and is well marked. Beware heavy wash from fishing boats. Also beware Digue Nord which partially cover at HW. Keep W and S of N light tower, Fl(2)R 6s.
LIGHTS AND MARKS
Ldg Lts 123° lead towards R Liane and marina. Besides normal traffic signals, special signals apply as follows:–

*G ⎫
W G ⎬ Movement suspended except for vessels with
R ⎭ special permission to enter

*G ⎫
WR ⎬ Movement suspended except for vessels with
R ⎭ special permission to leave inner and outer harbour

*G ⎫
W R ⎬ Movement suspended except for vessels with
R R ⎭ special permission to leave inner harbour

* Normal light signal prohibiting entry and departure.
Two Bu Lts (hor) mean sluicing from R Liane.
RADIO TELEPHONE
VHF Ch 12 16 (H24).
TELEPHONE (21)
Hr Mr 21.30.10.00; Hr Mr Plaisance 21.31.70.01; Harbour office 21.30.90.46; Aff Mar 21.30.53.23; CROSS 21.87.21.87; SNSM 21.31.42.59; # 21.30.14.24; Meteo 21.31.52.23; Auto 21.33.82.55; Police 21.31.75.17; Ⓗ 21.31.92.13; Brit Consul 21.30.25.11.
FACILITIES
Marina (350 + 50 visitors) ☎ 21.31.70.01, FW, Slip, AC, P, D, C (20 ton); **Quai Gambetta** M, P*, D*, L, FW, AB, V, R, Bar; **Baude Electronique** ☎ 21.30.01.15, Ⓔ; **Opale Marine** ☎ 21.30.36.19, ME, El, Sh, M, CH, Divers; **Angelo** ☎ 21.31.37.61, CH; **Librairie Duminy** ☎ 21.30.06.75, SHOM; **YC Boulonnais** ☎ 21.31.80.68, C, Bar. **Town** P, D, FW, ME, El, Sh, CH, V, Gaz, R, Bar. ⌂; Ⓑ; ⇌; ✈ (Le Touquet/Calais).
Ferry UK – Dover/Folkestone.
*Obtainable from Societé Maritime Carburante Liquide.

BOULOGNE *continued*

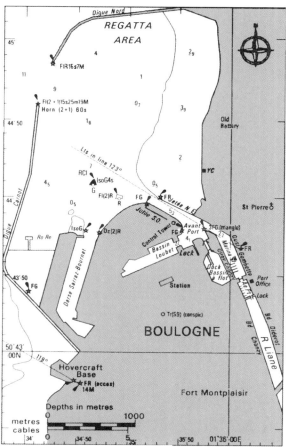

BOULOGNE

MINOR HARBOURS AND ANCHORAGES

ÉTAPLES, Pas de Calais, 5032'·00N, 01°38'·00E, Zone −0100, Admty chart 2451, SHOM 6795. HW 0000 on Dover + 0012 on Dieppe (zone − 0100); HW height −0·3m on Dieppe; ML 4·8m; Duration 0520. See 10.19.25. Very good shelter but entry to R Canche should not be attempted in strong on-shore winds. Access HW ∓ 2. Channel in river marked by posts between sunken training walls to Étaples, where shoal draft boats can lie afloat on pontoons at small marina just below the bridge. Alternatively yachts which can take the ground can dry out on sand opposite the YC at Le Touquet. Whole estuary dries. Camiers Lt Oc(2) WRG 6s 17m 9/6M. Facilities: Hr Mr ☎ 21.94.74.26; Aff Mar. ☎ 21.94.61.50. **Marina** (115 + 15 visitors), FW, C (3 ton), AC; **Quay C** (3 ton), FW, Slip; **Centre Nautique YC** ☎ 21.94.74.26. Bar, Slip; **Agence Nautique du Nord** ☎ 21.94.26.55. Ch, El, Ⓔ, M, ME, Sh; **ETS Lamour** ☎ 21.94.61.21, D; **Town** Ⓑ, Bar, D, P, ⌂; R, ⇌, V.
See also Le Touquet p82 for entrance.

LE TOUQUET
Pas De Calais

CHARTS
Admiralty 2451; SHOM 6795; ECM 1011; Stanford 1, 9; Imray C31

TIDES
Dover – 0010; ML 4·8; Duration 0520; Zone –0100

Standard Port DIEPPE

Times				Height (metres)			
HW		LW		MHWS	MHWN	MLWN	MLWS
0100	0600	0100	0700	9·3	7·2	2·6	0·7
1300	1800	1300	1900				

Differences LE TOUQUET (ETAPLES)

+0012	No data			–0·3	0·0	+0·1	+0·3

SHELTER
Good except in strong W winds. Yacht moorings, which dry, are to stbd after passing Pt de Touquet. There are plans to build a dam across the mouth of the R Canche, with locks. Marina at Étaples – see 10.19.29.

NAVIGATION
Waypoint 50°35'·00N 01°31'·80E, 308°/128° from/to Camiers Lt, 3·8M. Entrance is not easy – local pilots or fishermen are available. Best entrance is at HW – 1. In W winds the sea breaks heavily a long way out and entry should not be attempted. The channel is always changing and buoys are moved accordingly. Beware stranded wreck 2M NW of Le Touquet-Paris Plage Lt Ho, marked by Lt buoy.

LIGHTS AND MARKS
Good landmarks are the Terres de Tourmont, a conspic range 175m high, visible for 25 miles. Le Touquet is at the S end of this range. Entrance between Pt de Lornel and Pt de Touquet. Pick up buoyed channel in R section of Camiers Lt. Pt du Touquet light is Y tower, Brown band, W & G top – Fl (2) 10s 54m 25M.

RADIO TELEPHONE
VHF CH 21; 16.

TELEPHONE (21)
Hr Mr 21.05.12.77; Aff Mar Etaples 21.94.61.50; Auto 21.05.13.55; # 21.05.01.72; CROSS 21.87.21.87; Police 21.94.60.17; Dr 21.05.14.42; Brit Consul 21.96.33.76.

FACILITIES
Cercle Nautique du Touquet ☎ 21.05.12.77, Slip, M, P, ME, E, FW, C, CH, R, Bar: **Marina** (Etaples – See 10.19.29), AB, FW, P, D, AC; **Demoury** ☎ 21.84.51.76

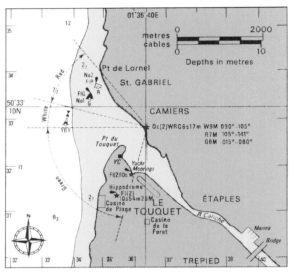

Sh, SM; **Technical Composite** Tel. 21.05.62.97, Sh. **Town** P, D, V, Gaz, R, Bar. PO; Bank; Rly; Air. Ferry UK – Boulogne – Dover/Folkestone.

Lights – distance off when rising or dipping (nautical miles)

Height of light						Height of eye					
		metres	1	2	3	4	5	6	7	8	9	10
metres	feet	feet	3	7	10	13	16	20	23	26	30	33
10	33		8.7	9.5	10.2	10.8	11.3	11.7	12.1	12.5	12.8	13.2
12	39		9.3	10.1	10.8	11.4	11.9	12.3	12.7	13.1	13.4	13.8
14	46		9.9	10.7	11.4	12.0	12.5	12.9	13.3	13.7	14.0	14.4
16	53		10.4	11.2	11.9	12.5	13.0	13.4	13.8	14.2	14.5	14.9
18	59		10.9	11.7	12.4	13.0	13.5	13.9	14.3	14.7	15.0	15.4
20	66		11.4	12.2	12.9	13.5	14.0	14.4	14.8	15.2	15.5	15.9
22	72		11.9	12.7	13.4	14.0	14.5	14.9	15.3	15.7	16.0	16.4
24	79		12.3	13.1	13.8	14.4	14.9	15.3	15.7	16.1	16.4	16.8
26	85		12.7	13.5	14.2	14.8	15.3	15.7	16.1	16.5	16.8	17.2
28	92		13.1	13.9	14.6	15.2	15.7	16.1	16.5	16.9	17.2	17.6
30	98		13.5	14.3	15.0	15.6	16.1	16.5	16.9	17.3	17.6	18.0
32	105		13.9	14.7	15.4	16.0	16.5	16.9	17.3	17.7	18.0	18.4
34	112		14.2	15.0	15.7	16.3	16.8	17.2	17.6	18.0	18.3	18.7
36	118		14.6	15.4	16.1	16.7	17.2	17.6	18.0	18.4	18.7	19.1
38	125		14.9	15.7	16.4	17.0	17.5	17.9	18.3	18.7	19.0	19.4
40	131		15.3	16.1	16.8	17.4	17.9	18.3	18.7	19.1	19.4	19.8
42	138		15.6	16.4	17.1	17.7	18.2	18.6	19.0	19.4	19.7	20.1
44	144		15.9	16.7	17.4	18.0	18.5	18.9	19.3	19.7	20.0	20.4
46	151		16.2	17.0	17.7	18.3	18.8	19.2	19.6	20.0	20.3	20.7
48	157		16.5	17.3	18.0	18.6	19.1	19.5	19.9	20.3	20.6	21.0
50	164		16.8	17.6	18.3	18.9	19.4	19.8	20.2	20.6	20.9	21.3
55	180		17.5	18.3	19.0	19.6	20.1	20.5	20.9	21.3	21.6	22.0
60	197		18.2	19.0	19.7	20.3	20.8	21.2	21.6	22.0	22.3	22.7
65	213		18.9	19.7	20.4	21.0	21.5	21.9	22.3	22.7	23.0	23.4
70	230		19.5	20.3	21.0	21.6	22.1	22.5	22.9	23.2	23.6	24.0
75	246		20.1	20.9	21.6	22.2	22.7	23.1	23.5	23.9	24.2	24.6
80	262		20.7	21.5	22.2	22.8	23.3	23.7	24.1	24.5	24.8	25.2
85	279		21.3	22.1	22.8	23.4	23.9	24.3	24.7	25.1	25.4	25.8
90	295		21.8	22.6	23.3	23.9	24.4	24.8	25.2	25.6	25.9	26.3
95	312		22.4	23.2	23.9	24.5	25.0	25.4	25.8	26.2	26.5	26.9
metres	feet	metres	1	2	3	4	5	6	7	8	9	10
Height of light		feet	3	7	10	13	16	20	23	26	30	33
							Height of eye					

ENGLAND, SOUTH COAST — DOVER
Lat 51°07' N Long 1°19' E
TIMES AND HEIGHTS OF HIGH AND LOW WATERS

TIME ZONE UT (GMT)
Summer Time add ONE hour in non-shaded area

MAY

Day	Time	m	Time	m	Time	m	Time	m
1 F	0327	1.2	0826	6.0	1553	1.2	2049	6.3
2 Sa	0424	0.8	0912	6.4	1647	0.9	2135	6.6
3 Su	0516	0.6	0957	6.6	1736	0.7	2220	6.8
4 M ●	0604	0.5	1044	6.8	1821	0.6	2306	6.9
5 Tu	0649	0.4	1133	6.8	1904	0.5	2354	6.9
6 W	0733	0.4	1224	6.8	1949	0.5		
7 Th	0043	6.8	0818	0.5	1314	6.6	2034	0.6
8 F	0133	6.5	0904	0.7	1402	6.4	2124	0.8
9 Sa	0223	6.2	0955	1.1	1450	6.1	2216	1.2
10 Su	0318	5.9	1051	1.5	1545	5.8	2318	1.5
11 M	0421	5.5	1157	1.7	1651	5.5		
12 Tu	0027	1.6	0544	5.3	1309	1.9	1812	5.4
13 W	0142	1.6	0713	5.4	1423	1.8	1928	5.6
14 Th	0256	1.5	0816	5.6	1529	1.6	2025	5.8
15 F	0357	1.3	0901	5.8	1624	1.4	2110	6.0
16 Sa	0447	1.2	0939	5.9	1706	1.3	2149	6.2
17 Su	0525	1.1	1013	6.1	1740	1.2	2226	6.3
18 M	0556	1.1	1048	6.2	1807	1.1	2302	6.4
19 Tu ○	0624	1.0	1122	6.3	1838	1.0	2336	6.4
20 W	0656	0.9	1154	6.3	1912	1.0		
21 Th	0005	6.3	0730	0.9	1224	6.3	1947	1.0
22 F	0031	6.2	0804	0.9	1252	6.2	2022	1.1
23 Sa	0057	6.1	0839	1.1	1323	6.1	2056	1.3
24 Su	0131	5.9	0912	1.3	1359	5.9	2134	1.4
25 M	0215	5.7	0952	1.5	1449	5.8	2216	1.6
26 Tu	0314	5.5	1040	1.7	1550	5.6	2309	1.7
27 W	0430	5.4	1139	1.8	1705	5.6		
28 Th	0017	1.7	0550	5.5	1250	1.8	1819	5.7
29 F	0135	1.5	0657	5.7	1406	1.6	1923	6.0
30 Sa	0247	1.2	0755	6.0	1512	1.3	2018	6.3
31 Su	0349	1.0	0847	6.3	1612	1.1	2108	6.5

JUNE

Day	Time	m	Time	m	Time	m	Time	m
1 M	0444	0.8	0938	6.5	1705	0.9	2159	6.7
2 Tu ●	0537	0.6	1028	6.6	1757	0.7	2248	6.8
3 W	0629	0.6	1120	6.7	1848	0.7	2339	6.8
4 Th	0721	0.6	1212	6.7	1938	0.6		
5 F	0031	6.7	0811	0.6	1300	6.6	2027	0.7
6 Sa	0120	6.5	0900	0.8	1345	6.4	2118	0.8
7 Su	0208	6.2	0948	1.1	1430	6.2	2207	1.1
8 M	0257	5.9	1037	1.4	1519	6.0	2259	1.4
9 Tu	0353	5.7	1129	1.7	1617	5.8	2356	1.6
10 W	0459	5.4	1227	1.9	1723	5.6		
11 Th	0059	1.7	0617	5.4	1328	2.0	1836	5.6
12 F	0206	1.8	0724	5.4	1436	2.0	1940	5.7
13 Sa	0311	1.7	0819	5.6	1535	1.8	2033	5.9
14 Su	0402	1.6	0905	5.8	1620	1.7	2118	6.0
15 M	0442	1.4	0946	6.0	1658	1.5	2200	6.2
16 Tu	0518	1.3	1024	6.1	1734	1.3	2237	6.2
17 W ○	0554	1.1	1101	6.3	1814	1.1	2312	6.3
18 Th	0634	1.0	1133	6.3	1853	1.0	2343	6.2
19 F	0712	1.0	1205	6.3	1931	1.0		
20 Sa	0014	6.2	0748	1.0	1238	6.3	2006	1.1
21 Su	0048	6.2	0822	1.1	1313	6.3	2042	1.1
22 M	0126	6.1	0856	1.2	1352	6.2	2118	1.2
23 Tu	0211	6.0	0935	1.3	1437	6.1	2159	1.3
24 W	0304	5.8	1019	1.5	1532	5.9	2247	1.4
25 Th	0409	5.7	1111	1.6	1634	5.9	2346	1.5
26 F	0516	5.7	1214	1.7	1742	5.9		
27 Sa	0056	1.5	0624	5.8	1326	1.6	1848	6.0
28 Su	0208	1.4	0727	5.9	1437	1.5	1949	6.1
29 M	0317	1.2	0826	6.1	1542	1.3	2049	6.3
30 Tu	0420	1.1	0924	6.3	1644	1.1	2143	6.5

JULY

Day	Time	m	Time	m	Time	m	Time	m
1 W ●	0520	0.9	1020	6.5	1742	1.0	2238	6.6
2 Th	0621	0.8	1112	6.6	1839	0.8	2330	6.6
3 F	0716	0.8	1200	6.7	1933	0.7		
4 Sa	0019	6.6	0806	0.8	1243	6.6	2022	0.7
5 Su	0104	6.5	0851	0.9	1326	6.5	2107	0.8
6 M	0147	6.3	0934	1.1	1406	6.4	2150	1.0
7 Tu	0232	6.1	1012	1.4	1451	6.2	2231	1.3
8 W	0319	5.8	1049	1.7	1541	6.0	2313	1.6
9 Th	0414	5.6	1129	1.9	1637	5.8		
10 F	0000	1.8	0518	5.4	1214	2.2	1742	5.6
11 Sa	0052	2.0	0631	5.3	1310	2.3	1853	5.5
12 Su	0157	2.1	0738	5.4	1420	2.2	1957	5.6
13 M	0304	1.9	0834	5.6	1529	2.0	2050	5.7
14 Tu	0359	1.7	0921	5.8	1623	1.7	2135	5.9
15 W	0445	1.5	1002	6.0	1709	1.4	2214	6.0
16 Th	0530	1.2	1037	6.2	1754	1.2	2247	6.2
17 F ○	0614	1.1	1109	6.3	1836	1.1	2319	6.3
18 Sa	0655	1.0	1143	6.5	1914	1.0	2354	6.3
19 Su	0733	1.0	1218	6.5	1954	0.9		
20 M	0032	6.4	0806	1.0	1257	6.5	2027	0.9
21 Tu	0114	6.4	0839	1.0	1338	6.4	2101	1.0
22 W	0159	6.3	0915	1.1	1420	6.3	2141	1.1
23 Th	0249	6.1	0956	1.3	1510	6.2	2224	1.2
24 F	0343	6.0	1044	1.5	1604	6.0	2316	1.4
25 Sa	0444	5.8	1142	1.7	1708	5.9		
26 Su	0021	1.6	0551	5.7	1252	1.8	1818	5.8
27 M	0137	1.6	0703	5.7	1411	1.7	1930	5.8
28 Tu	0256	1.5	0815	5.9	1527	1.5	2039	6.0
29 W	0409	1.3	0922	6.1	1634	1.3	2142	6.2
30 Th	0516	1.1	1017	6.4	1737	1.1	2235	6.4
31 F ●	0619	1.0	1102	6.5	1835	0.9	2322	6.5

AUGUST

Day	Time	m	Time	m	Time	m	Time	m
1 Sa	0713	0.9	1144	6.7	1927	0.8		
2 Su	0004	6.6	0759	0.9	1224	6.7	2011	0.7
3 M	0043	6.5	0837	0.9	1302	6.7	2050	0.8
4 Tu	0123	6.4	0910	1.1	1340	6.6	2124	1.0
5 W	0201	6.2	0936	1.4	1419	6.4	2155	1.3
6 Th	0243	6.0	1000	1.6	1501	6.2	2226	1.5
7 F	0328	5.7	1031	1.9	1549	5.9	2302	1.8
8 Sa	0421	5.4	1112	2.1	1645	5.5	2349	2.1
9 Su	0529	5.2	1205	2.4	1757	5.3		
10 M	0046	2.2	0650	5.1	1313	2.4	1917	5.2
11 Tu	0158	2.2	0801	5.3	1437	2.3	2020	5.4
12 W	0317	2.0	0853	5.6	1550	1.9	2110	5.6
13 Th	0416	1.7	0934	5.9	1644	1.5	2148	5.9
14 F	0506	1.3	1009	6.2	1733	1.2	2220	6.1
15 Sa ○	0554	1.1	1042	6.4	1818	1.0	2254	6.4
16 Su	0638	1.0	1118	6.6	1902	0.9	2332	6.5
17 M	0717	0.9	1156	6.7	1938	0.8		
18 Tu	0011	6.6	0749	0.9	1235	6.8	2009	0.8
19 W	0055	6.6	0819	0.9	1317	6.7	2042	0.8
20 Th	0138	6.5	0854	0.9	1359	6.6	2119	0.9
21 F	0226	6.3	0934	1.1	1446	6.3	2200	1.1
22 Sa	0317	6.1	1020	1.4	1538	6.1	2251	1.4
23 Su	0416	5.8	1115	1.7	1641	5.8	2357	1.7
24 M	0525	5.6	1229	1.9	1756	5.6		
25 Tu	0120	1.9	0648	5.5	1357	1.9	1923	5.6
26 W	0249	1.7	0816	5.7	1521	1.6	2047	5.8
27 Th	0406	1.5	0922	6.0	1633	1.3	2148	6.1
28 F	0515	1.2	1009	6.3	1734	1.0	2233	6.4
29 Sa ●	0614	1.0	1048	6.6	1829	0.8	2309	6.5
30 Su	0702	0.9	1125	6.7	1914	0.8	2344	6.5
31 M	0741	0.9	1201	6.8	1952	0.8		

TIDAL STREAMS

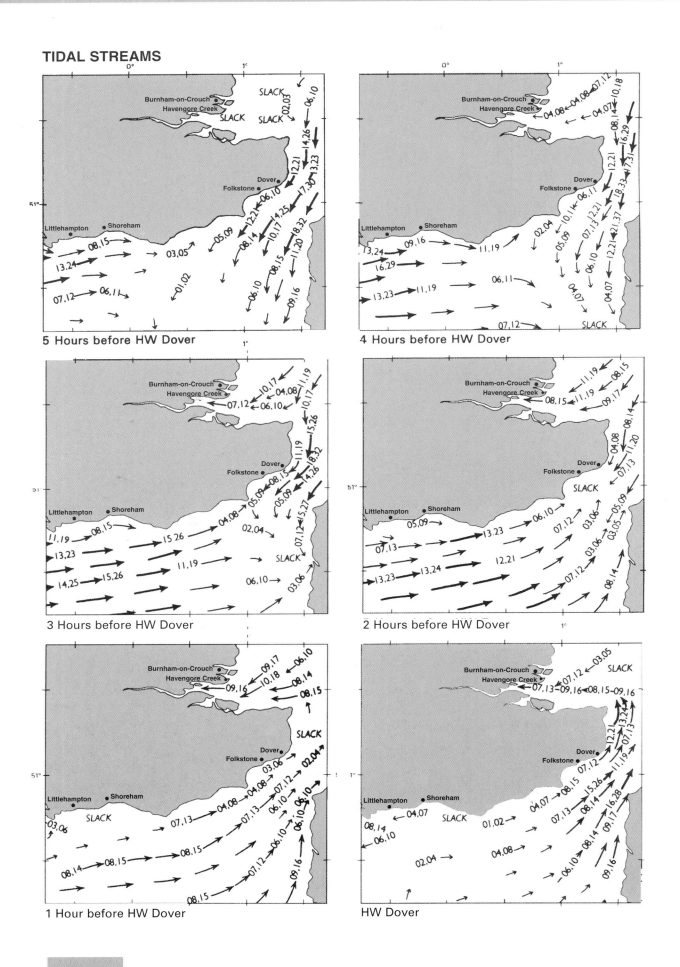

5 Hours before HW Dover

4 Hours before HW Dover

3 Hours before HW Dover

2 Hours before HW Dover

1 Hour before HW Dover

HW Dover

TIDAL STREAMS

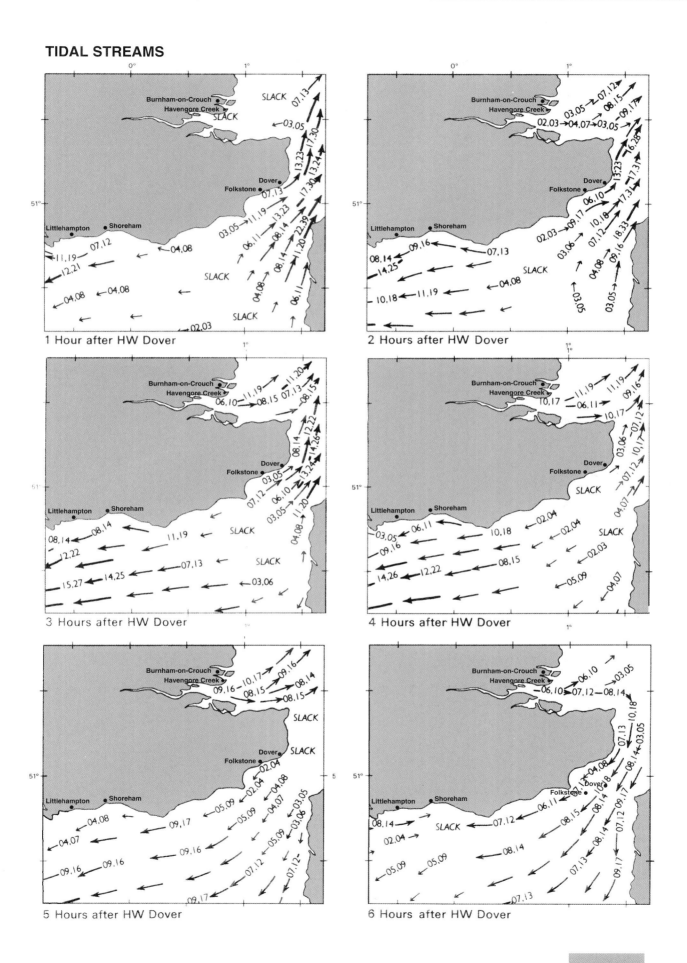

1 Hour after HW Dover

2 Hours after HW Dover

3 Hours after HW Dover

4 Hours after HW Dover

5 Hours after HW Dover

6 Hours after HW Dover

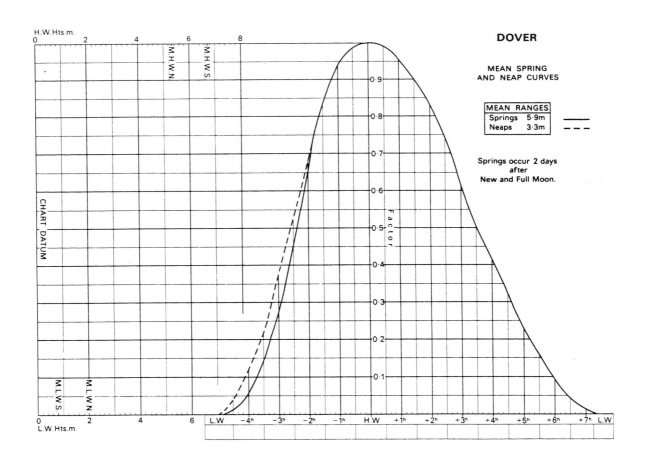

DOVER

MEAN SPRING
AND NEAP CURVES

MEAN RANGES	
Springs	5·9m ————
Neaps	3·3m – – –

Springs occur 2 days
after
New and Full Moon.

COMPASS DEVIATION TABLE

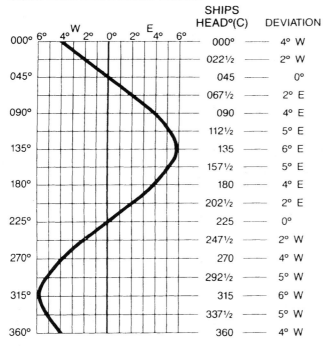

SHIPS HEAD°(C)	DEVIATION
000°	4° W
022½	2° W
045	0°
067½	2° E
090	4° E
112½	5° E
135	6° E
157½	5° E
180	4° E
202½	2° E
225	0°
247½	2° W
270	4° W
292½	5° W
315	6° W
337½	5° W
360	4° W

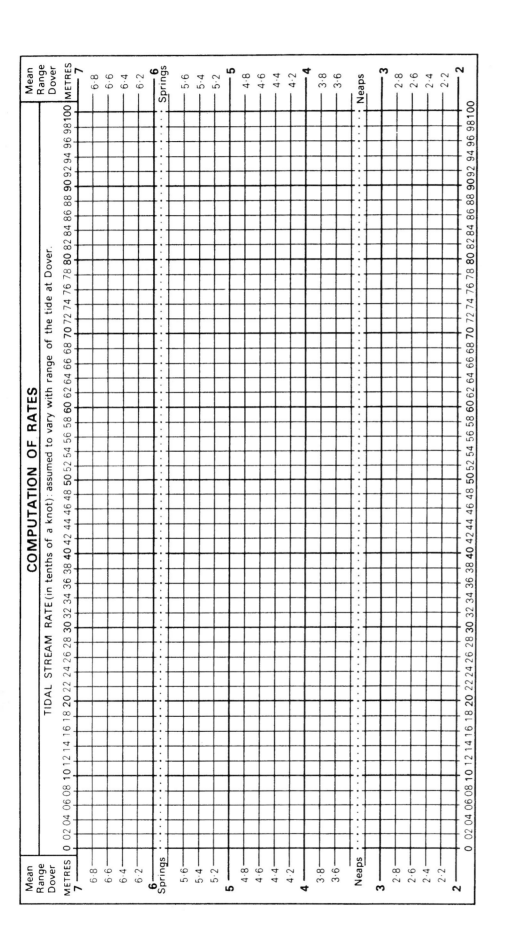

COMPUTATION OF RATES

TIDAL STREAM RATE (in tenths of a knot): assumed to vary with range of the tide at Dover.

Computation of Rates – Example

Required to predict the rate of tidal stream off Dungeness at 0630 on a day for which the tidal prediction for Dover is:

HW	0012	5.6m
LW	0643	0.4m
HW	1134	5.6m
LW	1906	0.4m

Mean Range of tide at Dover for the day is 5.2m and the appropriate chart in the atlas is that for **5 hours before HW Dover.**

This gives mean neap and spring rates for the required position (off Dungeness) of:

12, 21 (1.2kn, 2.1kn)

Enter the diagram Computation of Rates above with these mean neap and spring rates, joining the dots representing them with a ruler. From the intersection of this line with the horizontal line representing the range at Dover (5.2m) follow the line vertically to the scale of Tidal Stream Rates (top or bottom) and read off the predicted rate – in this example 1.9 knots.

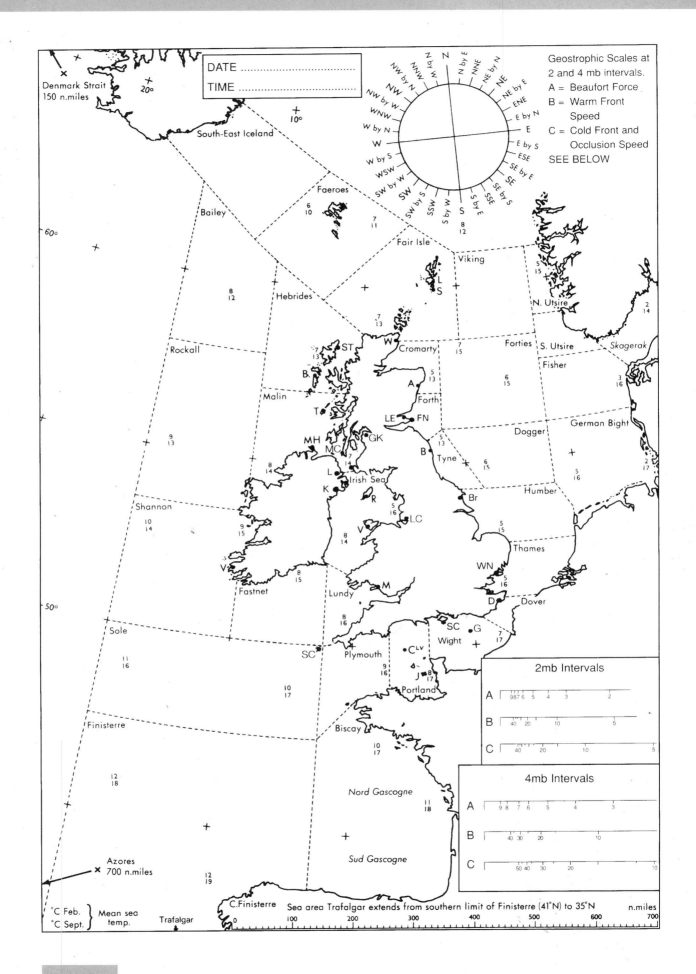

Denmark Strait
150 n.miles

South-East Iceland

DATE ....
TIME ....

Geostrophic Scales at
2 and 4 mb intervals.
A = Beaufort Force
B = Warm Front
    Speed
C = Cold Front and
    Occlusion Speed
SEE BELOW

Faeroes

Bailey

Fair Isle

Viking

N. Utsire

Hebrides

Cromarty

Forties

S. Utsire

Skagerak

Rockall

Fisher

Malin

Forth

Dogger

German Bight

LE   FN

Tyne

MH   MC

GK

L

Irish Sea

K

Humber

Shannon

R

Br

LC

V

Thames

Fastnet

M

WN

Lundy

D   Dover

Sole

SC   G

Wight

SC

Plymouth

C LV

J

Portland

Biscay

Finisterre

Nord Gascogne

Azores
700 n.miles

Sud Gascogne

°C Feb. } Mean sea
°C Sept. } temp.

Trafalgar

C.Finisterre   Sea area Trafalgar extends from southern limit of Finisterre (41°N) to 35°N   n.miles
0   100   200   300   400   500   600   700

2mb Intervals
A   9 8 7 6   5   4   3   2
B   40 20   10   5
C   40   20   10   5

4mb Intervals
A   9 8 7   6   5   4   3
B   40 30   20   10
C   50 40 30   20   10